# LOVE & LOSS

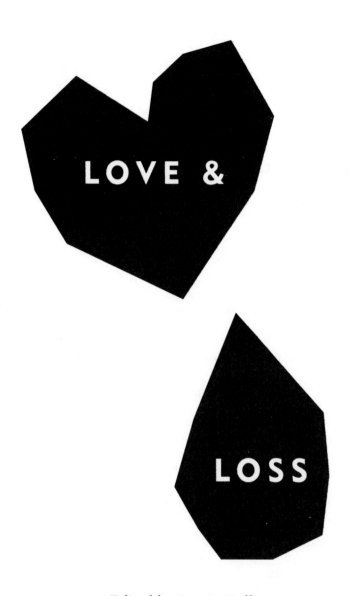

# LOVE &

# LOSS

Edited by Renée Hollis

# TIMELESS WISDOM

**True stories that reveal the depths of the human experience**

## Emotional Inheritance

First published 2020

Emotional Inheritance
An imprint of Exisle Publishing Pty Ltd
PO Box 864, Chatswood, NSW 2057, Australia
226 High Street, Dunedin, 9016, New Zealand
www.exislepublishing.com

A CiP record for this book is available from the National Library of Australia.

ISBN 978-1-925820-07-2

Designed by Nada Backovic
Typeset in 12/18 Sabon Lt Std
Printed in China

This book uses paper sourced under ISO 14001 guidelines from well-managed forests and other controlled sources.

10 9 8 7 6 5 4 3 2 1

My thoughts go out to you,
my Immortal Beloved.
I can live only wholly with
you or not at all —
Be calm, my life, my all.
Only by calm consideration
of our existence
can we achieve our purpose
to live together.
Oh continue to love me,
never misjudge
the most faithful heart of your beloved.
Ever thine.
Ever mine.
Ever ours.

**LUDWIG VAN BEETHOVEN**

# CONTENTS

Grief is like the ocean; it comes in waves, ebbing and flowing. Sometimes the water is calm, and sometimes it is overwhelming. All we can do is learn to swim.

VICKI HARRISON

# INTRODUCTION

Every day in the news we hear remarkable true stories that demonstrate the resilience of the human spirit. We thought it was time that more of these stories were heard, so we organized an international short story writing competition, which has resulted in the publication of the *Timeless Wisdom* collection of books.

We were overwhelmed by the variety and richness of the hundreds of entries from around the world. Our criteria for final selection were that the stories should reflect a diversity of writing, blend humour and pathos, and balance moments of drama with those of quiet contemplation.

Love and loss are polar opposites, from euphoria to deep sorrow. But both emotions can encompass intense feelings of affection, fondness, tenderness, warmth and endearment. In this book, mature writers share their life experiences of love and loss with honesty, humour and a unique insight that we can all learn from. From a daughter caring for her father with Alzheimer's, to a man's reflections on his young biracial romance; from a woman coping with the aftermath of a terrible accident and death of a close friend, to another contemplating the parts of her that are lost after migrating from her homeland — these are stories of unexpected love and loss that had a lasting impact on the storyteller. The stories are interspersed with quotes about love and loss by people as diverse as Dr Seuss, John Lennon, Ludwig van Beethoven, John Green and Michael Caine. The result is a book that explores all that is best about human nature.

# HUNADI' A HLABIRWA

## Pheladi Makgeru

The soil in my backyard is fertile, rich and a good enough brown to plant my fruit there. I always water my fruit so the loose soil doesn't expose it to the harsh sun. I make sure the soil forms a clay before I leave; it is part of the ritual. Today I bury the seventh. I am a gardener, one more familiar with loss than growth, but I am optimistic.

The water in my worn yellow *atchaar* (a raw pickled mango treat) bucket is glistening too brightly. It reminds of the river across from my home and how it mocks us after it swallows another child alive.

I am kneeling on my dusty black gardening cloth. It needs washing or else people might mistake it for soil. My husband normally comes back when the sun shies away into the mountain pockets for refuge. Today there is no sun, the sky is coloured with a saddening umber. He is late, or maybe he is waiting for the sun to dip into the horizon before he comes back. The sun is replaced by a dark gloom, which makes the village look like a deadly hallow.

We live in a semi-arid land, right by the Tropic of Capricorn in one of the hottest regions in South Africa. We pray for the rain here and water is an expensive commodity. It hardly rains, but when it does disaster follows. The mountain behind my home is slowly darkened by the thick dreary clouds covering us. I should have planted my fruit deeper; if the rain comes it will be exposed. I saw men with guns scurry across the dry river the other day. They were from out of town, white men, and they were carrying the bodies of dead boys who they had shot down. The land is obviously mourning today. It is the only time the skies will grow grey.

There are no stars tonight, just lightning and tranquility. My husband is still not back. He is the son of a chief, tall, fair skinned and funny. He rarely smiles, he wears worry as loudly as he wears his pride. I wish I knew what he was thinking half of the time he lies beside me. On most days we lie on the mattress or the cold floor to get lost in each other's gaze. I always dismiss his sadness with thoughts that he is a busy man — he will be chief one day and that on its own would drive any man to a special kind of misery.

He built our home five years before I gave birth to our second child. A four-roomed maroon house, with a fancy iron roof and enclosed pit toilets. I would like to think that we were the envy of many; we had visitors almost every day. Many would admire the shimmer of our roof and the unusual colour of our walls. The common house would be made of mud or makeshift bricks made by the young men down in the valley. My husband would always tell them that he only had to have the best, he was a royal man after all. I found that funny. Many found him cocky for that, but I guess my sense of humour stretched out to accommodate his pride.

By the time I had birthed him the fifth child, we had ten cows to each in our *kraal*. I remember how he would count them loudly with the usual hint of pride in his voice. He had gone to school when the missionaries came to our village, and would speak in English every time we were entertaining guests. One time he read them a story. I barely remember the contents of it, although I remember how he would read 'of course' with a curl in his 'r'. I learnt a bit of English from when he put on shows for local men and our children in the yard, or every time he would forget his books. I never went to school — it was a privilege reserved for men, especially men like him.

The silence in this house is haunting. My husband hasn't graced me with his presence yet (he would probably say that to make me smile). The rain is heavy, I worry for him, and on days like this the river is merciless. He has to cross it every time he comes back from the royal house. In the midst of all the thunder and raindrop clanks on my roof, I hear the slam of the gate. We have a metal one, so I can hear any activity that involves it. The slam was too violent to be my husband's.

He always closes the gate gently, even when it is raining. He handles everything delicately. He is going to be a good chief.

A ten-year-old adorned with mucus on his face is at my doorstep, knocking with a sense of urgency. He looks like he's been cleaned up by the rain and seemingly untethered by it. He tells me his father stripped his clothes off and let the river take him. The ten-year-old has the clothes in a tight grip on his chest. I can't tell where his tears start and where the rain ends on his cheeks.

He is my son.

I wanted to tell my husband about the seventh fruit I buried today. His name was Kgagudi. I buried him next to the *kraal*, like the other six. He let the river take him. Maybe he wanted to get closer to his children — he was always one to want to feel other people's pain. If the river brings him back, I will bury him next to his children.

Hlabirwa' a Ngwato

Attitude is a choice.
Happiness is a choice.
Optimism is a choice.
Kindness is a choice.
Giving is a choice.
Respect is a choice.
Whatever choice you
make makes you.
Choose wisely.

**ROY T. BENNETT**

# FAIRY GODMOTHERS

## Maria Nolan

Everyone should have one, you know ... a fairy godmother.

They're magic! They have the ability to change lives and every life needs changing at some time or other, regardless of how perfect it seems.

I first met mine when I was nine years old. It was 1966 and I, being the eldest, was the one designated to collect Marie Harrison-East from the Rosslare train, my parents being far too occupied running our public house to go traipsing after foreign visitors on a busy Saturday afternoon.

'Mind you wash your hands and face and put something clean on and don't go making a holy show of us,' were my only instructions.

Marie Harrison-East, a romantic and exciting name to my nine-year-old imagination.

I had heard it mentioned several times between my mam and my Aunt Peg over the years. She was a second cousin of theirs on the MacDonald side and had been home for both their weddings but not since. A single lady 'doing quite well for herself working for Barclays Bank in London' and we, it seemed, were her only relations.

Daydreaming, I reached the station just in time to see a vision of loveliness alighting from one of the carriages that I knew instinctively to be Marie Harrison-East. Tall, blonde and beautiful … all that a fairy godmother should be. I can still see her standing there all these years later, white dress sprinkled with delicate pink roses, sweetheart neckline, tightly clinched at the waist falling into full skirt, pretty white peep-toe shoes, delicate lace gloves, white handbag and a string of pearls, looking like every movie star I had ever seen on the big screen. She was stunning and I was stunned. Little did I know my stunning was far from over, as right behind her appeared the most handsome man I had ever seen in all of my young life. Dark haired, tanned, sporting a well-groomed moustache, he wore a beautifully tailored charcoal grey suit, pristine white shirt and a cravat of all things — Rhett Butler eat your heart out.

'Are you Marie Harrison-East?' I enquired in a timid voice, not sure if she could hear me as she searched the station for a familiar face.

'Why yes I am,' she replied. 'And this is my friend Mr King,' indicating the attractive man still standing behind her. 'And who might you be?'

I am certain now that both Marie and Mr King were surprised that I was the one sent to fetch them, and I would say even more surprised to find that they were going to have to walk all the way across town carrying their own suitcases. We did have one hackney car in Enniscorthy in those days but I wouldn't have had an idea how to go about getting it. I told them that it wasn't far to walk, which it wasn't for a nine-year-old with no heels and no bags to carry.

When we came to the Portsmouth Arms Hotel, Mr King said that he thought they should take me in for a bowl of ice-cream as a treat for coming to meet them. My siblings would be green with envy when I told them. I had strawberry and vanilla ice-cream in a stainless steel bowl — I was theirs forever.

I often wonder why that afternoon has stood out in my childhood memory as one of the most significant of my life. Sitting in the plush surroundings of the Portsmouth Arms, I think I caught my first glimpse of 'being in love' and I think I have been in love with the feeling ever since! That wonderful time in a relationship when all is new and exciting and cloud nine is not quite high enough for floating on.

I didn't want that afternoon to end — ever. And I certainly didn't want to take this beautiful couple home to waste their magic on people I felt sure wouldn't have any time for that 'ould carry on'.

There was nothing romantic about 1966 rural Ireland and 'that ould carry on' only went on in the films. It wasn't real — there was no such thing and 'young girls would want to get those queer notions out of their heads and do something useful for a change'.

But it didn't only happen in the films. There I was looking at it right now before my very eyes. As we prepared to leave the hotel, a feeling of sadness and foreboding came over me and I was quite certain that the spell was about to be broken. How right I was. My mother and my aunt were quite shocked to see Marie arrive with a man; after all, she hadn't mentioned it when she had written. After the introductions and the minimum of niceties Marie was ushered into the kitchen for what I knew was going to be a grilling. They would want to know everything about Mr King and they would get it out of her one way or another. She would be no match for them — they were like the Gestapo when they were looking for information, sure didn't I know well.

I was never told exactly what went on in the kitchen that day, but it appears Mr King and Marie had known each other for some time. But they had no plans to marry as Mr King had been married before, divorced, and not really in too much hurry to do the same again. But they were enjoying being together and had been looking forward to a few days in Ireland with relations.

Well, they were told there was no room at the inn for Mr King, so he would just have to book a room for himself in one of the town's hotels.

Marie's suggestion that they would both get a room at the hotel was shot down immediately — she would do no such thing. Sure hadn't they told half the town that she was coming over to stay with them and besides it wouldn't look right — after all, this was Enniscorthy not London!

Poor Marie, the London sophisticate, defeated by small town morals and rural narrow mindedness.

That day in 1966 my life changed forever.

Mr King booked into Murphy Floods Hotel and Marie stayed with us, and the rest of the week was quite strained. Because Mr King had been married before and was a divorcee, no one liked him. Oh, and he was a Protestant as well, which did nothing to improve his popularity. I decided there and then to take people as I found them and mind my own business when it came to their past.

At the end of the week Mr King returned to England and we never saw him again. Thankfully, I cannot say the same for my fairy godmother, who continued to keep in touch with us over the ensuing years through letters, photographs and postcards from all over the world. But never once returned to Ireland during this time.

Before my 21st birthday I decided that I would very much like to invite Marie Harrison-East to join us for the celebrations. Lo and behold I had a prompt reply saying that she would be delighted.

It was 1978 and not much had changed in Enniscorthy, I mused, as I waited for the Rosslare train to pull into the station. Marie, too, had changed little, looking elegant in a lilac suit with a pencil skirt and peplum jacket, her luxurious blonde hair swept back into a neat chignon at the nape of her neck, topped by a cream pillbox hat with gossamer-like lace just shading her eyes, cream gloves, cream shoes and cream bag. At 57 she was still very much a stunner. But this time there was no attractive man standing behind her and as she scanned the platform I couldn't help the sad feeling that enveloped me.

I asked her if she would like to take a taxi (Enniscorthy having improved slightly) but she said she would prefer to walk, even though this time both of us were in heels. When we came to the Portsmouth Arms Hotel she stopped and said 'Shall we?' I laughed and said, 'Only if I can have pink and white ice-cream in a stainless steel bowl.'

Over the course of the afternoon we laughed and talked and shared our life stories but Mr King was never mentioned, nor her last visit to Ireland.

When we rose to leave, she gently touched my arm. 'Promise me,' she said, 'that you will always do what your heart desires and not what other people expect you to do,' and she placed a small black ring box in my hand. Inside there was a beautiful sapphire ring encrusted with diamonds.

'For your 21st,' she said smiling. 'I know Mr King would want you to have it.'

The **most important** work you will ever do will be within the walls of your own home.

HAROLD B. LEE

# THANKS MUM

## Madeleine McDonald

Mum came to the rescue, as mums do. I felt ill the entire time I was pregnant: exhausted, headachy and listless. I even felt ill for two weeks before I knew I was pregnant. Unwilling to swallow medication, I decided the only way to cope was to batten down the hatches, eat sensibly and wait.

Mum came for a long visit because my husband was away serving in the army. A few days after her arrival, reassured that nothing was seriously wrong with me, she got the vacuum cleaner out. In my groggy state, I had not vacuumed for weeks and it showed. 'It's like mowing the lawn,' she chirped. 'I'm leaving stripes in the carpet.' Her tone was cheerful, as if inviting me to come and admire a flower that had just unfurled its petals in her much-loved garden.

That was Mum. Zero interest in hygiene or housework.

As teenagers, my brother and I took Mum's services for granted. It never occurred to me she would not down tools to help me with maths homework or to unpick a zip I had sewn in wrong. Her help was freely given, albeit underpinned by the conviction that she knew best.

My brother and I, self-absorbed brats, muttered that she should get a job and stop trying to run (or was that ruin?) our lives. I wish I could go back and apologize. Back then, I really thought she had made a deliberate choice to be a stay-at-home mother, a situation I intended to avoid.

In my twenties I read Betty Friedan and Gloria Steinem. Only then did I understand the frustration of a generation of clever women who had done their bit in the war, from driving tractors to code-breaking. Never mind the youth they lost and the skills they gained, the returning menfolk needed jobs, and women were herded back to the kitchen sink.

Dad, lovely man though he was, would have crawled over broken glass rather than send his wife out to work. Male pride was at stake. Thus Mum, intellectually curbed, turned her energies to gardening and interfering in other people's lives. Housework came low on the list.

As children, my brother and I once went to bed while visitors were still in the house. 'My bed's not made!' my brother bellowed. Sudden silence from the grown-ups and our embarrassed mother shot upstairs to remedy this. As a child, I didn't understand why Dad, coming to bid us goodnight, commented that it might have been worse: he could have shouted 'My bed's made!' We were inured to Mum's minimal standards — although we kids, Dad and no doubt their visitors all assumed it was a mother's job to rectify the situation. Another thing I never understood as a child was why Mum popped across the road to Leah's house for a cup of tea and a chat, but Leah was never offered tea in ours. 'She's Jewish,' Mum explained, with the same tolerant bemusement she displayed towards Quakers or vegetarians. 'That means she's not allowed to drink out of my cups — and don't bother her with questions about it.' When I got married, Leah gave me a cookbook of traditional Jewish recipes. Reading the fearsome instructions on keeping a kosher kitchen, which included scrubbing the pantry shelves once a fortnight, I saw her reluctance to drink from Mum's cups in a new light. For dogs, cats and chickens ambled in and out of our kitchen. When we were little, Mum sometimes carried the kitchen table out into the garden and turned it upside down so that my brother and I could play at going to sea in a boat.

Despite the lack of hygiene, she fed us plentifully. A proper cooked meal made its appearance on the table ten minutes after Dad arrived home from work. Sad to say, in 46 years of marriage she never made any effort to extend her culinary repertoire. Like it or lump it, three times a week we sat down to stew and dumplings, a cheap cut of meat simmered with barley and whatever vegetables were in season. Dad, who could not fry an egg, ate everything put in front of him, and rubbed his stomach with satisfaction. His greatest compliment was to say, 'That was a belly stretcher.'

In my travelling years, I attempted to introduce my parents to the delights of side salads, fruit for dessert or yoghurt to complement curry. They both took tiny mouthfuls before rejecting dubious foreign fare.

Content with his lot, Dad shrugged off my mother's lack of domestic skills and told us he had been warned by his future father-in-law. The older man had told him, 'You'll be sewing your own buttons on, laddie.'

In my twenties and thirties, I foisted feminist books and tracts on Mum, convinced she would agree with their message.

To my surprise, she shook her head and assured me women obtained better results by guile than by confrontation. Hah! That was advice I had no intention of heeding. I revelled in the fact that my generation overturned the old stereotypes and did things differently. I did, however, emulate her splendid disregard for domesticity. Housework was low on the list of my priorities.

It took marriage to an army-trained medic, who disinfected surfaces with bleach, to improve my lax standards. However, the appearance of the bleach bottles marked the beginning of a long-running battle between us. The theory that when both spouses work for pay they also share the housework crashed into the buffers of reality. I don't enjoy cleaning, but I do know all chores have to be done sooner or later. My husband, on the other hand, has chores he deems necessary, such as disinfecting the kitchen and bathroom, and others he point-blank refuses to touch until I resort to blackmail. It has taken years of bickering to reach a compromise.

Long ago, reading a litany of articles by exasperated feminists on the theme of 'What women need is a wife', I came to realize that what I needed, what I still need, what everybody needs, is a mum. An unsung heroine to step in and do the donkey work without complaint. More than that, everybody needs to feel there is someone on their side, right or wrong, someone who can then put petty disagreements and upsets into perspective.

Life goes forwards, not backwards. Like others before me, it was only when I became a mother myself that I understood and valued everything she did for us. I still miss her. Finding my own way through the messy, competing demands of family life, I keep her cheerful example in mind and often apologize to her shade. There is nothing that mums will not do for their children. Mine even overcame the aversion of a lifetime to set to and vacuum my carpet.

To a father
growing old,
nothing is dearer
than a daughter.

**EURIPIDES**

# GOING HOME

## K.W. George

Driving to the retirement home I pass a schoolboy walking along the pavement. He's gangly, dressed in grey serge shorts with his shirt hanging out, a backpack hoisted over one red-blazered shoulder. He's staring into the distance, probably thinking of some girl, or some wave he might catch later this afternoon in this seaside town at the bottom of Africa. I think of how little this boy knows of his future. Of what's to come. Of the years stretching ahead. The fears and the challenges, the joy. I think of the man lying in Frail Care in the retirement home who is at the other end of his life, and how limited this boy's knowledge is, of how he will grow old ... shuffling with his walker to the bathroom in his shabby slippers and his threadbare bathrobe.

❀

I stand over the hand basin cleaning my father's false teeth. His room in Frail Care is pokey compared to the large and rambling house he shared with Mum. The bedcovers, bold stripes of navy, red and white, were cheap, purchased for brightness not durability. In a cupboard, alongside a white bedside table, are my dad's few pieces of clothing. A green plastic mug squats on the windowsill.

There's a commode, and a window overlooking a parking lot. In the distance, a view of the mountain.

As a child, I saw these dentures in the morning, grinning at me from a glass of water in the bathroom. They have firm, pink gums — not what I was expecting. I clean away fragments of apple using the toothbrush. When I come to ease the teeth back into my dad's mouth he raises his eyebrows in alarm. They're upside-down! Mortified, I look at my father, and he gives me a little smile.

It's a little smile because everything about him is diminished. From his voice to his stature, he has withered away. In bed, he takes up as much room as a child. Even his penis has shrunk, and from the moment I visit him in Frail Care this problem is a preoccupation. 'I'm so glad you're here,' he murmurs. 'I need — I need …' And he explains to me that he cannot get his short member into the urine bottle without spilling. The messing embarrasses him. Understandably. So it is I find myself in a pharmacy asking for a urine bottle with a long neck or some kind of extension. I use my hands to gesticulate. 'We don't stock such a thing,' the pharmacist tells me.

'What we have is a penile sheath, which is like a condom tapering off to an opening, which makes it all much more manageable. Does your dad need small, medium or large?'

Mum has surprised me. All her married life Dad managed their finances. Now, suddenly, she has to roll over fixed deposits, write cheques and navigate ATMs. On one occasion, long before I arrive, she even chops wood for the fire. But she is amazingly resilient. I tell her this one day in the car. 'You're so strong,' I say. 'I haven't seen you shed a single tear.'

'You've just arrived,' she says. 'You forget I've been watching your father deteriorate for months. He's not the man I knew.'

He's not the man I knew, either. The father I knew as a teenager regularly told me I would never amount to anything. The father I knew whacked me on the side of the head without warning when I was outspoken or rebellious. He embarrassed me by entering a darkened dance hall where I was entwined in the arms of a boy, and switching on the lights, demanding that I leave. Now.

When my own children were born, he criticized them. He said they were soft and badly disciplined, and that my four year old needed a good thrashing. These things happened a long time ago and I have forgiven him. I forgave him because he served on Royal Navy destroyers in World War II when he was sixteen. I forgave him because he saw things no kid of sixteen should witness, and almost certainly these were things he could not unsee.

The man in Frail Care is kind and gentle, and doesn't lose his temper. He's not arrogant any more, either, but his mind is wandering. One afternoon, we sit in the sun on the balcony. Dad wears his red-checked flannel shirt, his worn and faded naval cap with the gold braid, and rests his claw-like hands in his lap. On his feet are shabby slippers. I've suggested replacing them but he's told me, 'My slippers are tatty. I am tatty. If you don't like it, you can shove off.'

'Do you see those little birds,' he says to me now, 'hovering above the golf course?' I don't, but I say 'Hmm' anyway. I see the silvery corrugated iron roof of the retirement home and, beyond that, the red tiles of the village houses and, further still, the rust-coloured rocky outcrop of the mountain. Above it all, the blue sky. Clear and calm. Unruffled by feathers.

'Those little guys,' he gestures with one gnarled finger, 'they hover up there, then they suddenly drop their wings and plummet to the ground.' He looks at me as if this feat is worth consideration. 'When they reach the ground,' he goes on, 'they pick up their wings again, and soar upwards, all shiny and bright. It's amazing,' he says in wonder.

I have no idea what he's talking about, but I love the sound of it.

Another time I slip quietly into his room in the early afternoon. He's flat on his back, his head and arms stuck inside his stretched-to-breaking-point T-shirt. He flails his legs and grunts, fighting to free himself. I don't know how long he's been like this.

The buzzer is out of reach.

'Oh, thank you,' he gasps, his face mottled with exertion, his emaciated ribcage heaving, when I help him. 'I'm so glad you're here.'

Once, I don't manage to visit him in the morning, because this is the day after my mother falls, which is a whole other story of ambulances and emergency rooms and no sleep. When I reach him in the afternoon, he looks at me accusingly. 'I could've done with you this morning.' He raises his hands feebly. 'Where were you? I've been frantic. I don't know where your mother is.'

Later, he forgets she's had a fall, and asks why she hasn't come to visit, and when I gently remind him, he grimaces in frustration and says, 'Oh, yes, that's right.'

❄

The day before I am due to fly home to Australia, I find him in a bad way.

Every now and then he stops breathing and drifts off, then jerks awake, wide-eyed and confused, gasping for breath like a fish out of water. People tiptoe in and out — his carers, the matron, a nurse who has grown particularly fond of him. Once, he raises my hand to his lips and kisses it. Another time he rambles on about a Canadian destroyer in the war that went down, and the injustice of the crew being forgotten to history. He wants these sailors mentioned at his funeral. He insists on it.

Finally, when the darkness outside his window is complete, he settles into semi peace, and I lean over and kiss his forehead before leaving.

During the night I wake several times, and lie waiting for the phone to ring, for the announcement of his death. I worry about the expense of the plane ticket that will have to be changed, and my family back home. When the sky lightens, I slip out of the house and walk down to the beach, and it's one of the most spectacular sunrises I have seen in a long time. The sky is several shades of pearl shot through with gold and rust. Low tide exposes a wide swathe of cold, wet sand at my feet. Seagulls wade wetly in the water. The waves whisper Has he? And then, Hasn't he? And I am convinced that my mother and cousin will have risen, be making phone calls informing friends and family of my father's demise. But when I reach home and click the garden gate behind me, walk up the pathway with sandy feet, the house is silent — everybody is still in bed.

After I have packed, I make a last-minute trip to the retirement home to say goodbye and find Dad sitting in his wheelchair on the balcony in the sun.

'I know what's happening today.' He looks hard at me. 'You're going home.'

I sit down beside him and take his rough and creased hand. I can't help thinking that he has made a special effort to pull himself together — just for me. If he can do so, so can I. I hold the tears at bay. I hold them back until he says, 'Could I also go home, please?'

Being deeply loved by someone gives you strength, while loving someone deeply gives you courage.

**LAO TZU**

# AN ORDINARY WOMAN

## Karen Elizabeth Lee

'Your mother has stage four cancer. It's treatable but not curable,' the doctor reassured us, her children. Every chemo treatment left her weak, confused, nauseous and with an inability to find the toilet when she needed it.

Mom had become thin, grey and fragile. She rarely ventured from her living room couch — too weak to climb the stairs to her bedroom, unable to boil water for her tea or push the lever down on the toaster.

That October, I made the journey to Ontario for the third time in six weeks. Most days, if I wasn't out buying groceries to make meals for the two of us, I sat reading in Dad's chair. Like Dad when he'd been alive, I became Mom's silent companion. Now, it was just me.

We had moved into this century home when I was eight. It is one of the oldest in the county, built on land given to an English sea captain in the late 1700s. He never visited the property, preferring to sell it to the family that eventually sold the house and 12 acres of land to our family.

The house is a traditional saltbox design, containing large rooms with built-in cupboards, 8-foot ceilings, and polished pine floors, but the kitchen and bathroom desperately needed upgrading and the mice laughed as I tried to interrupt their indoor antics and show them the door. It's perched on a hill, surrounded by green fields interwoven by dirt roads that lead to small villages, with a view of blue lake water in the far distance. Spruce, birch, catalpa, apple and black walnut trees had, over the years, been strategically planted on the property in between gooseberry and lilac bushes. Mom had added a flower and shrub garden around two sides of the house after Dad passed away.

No one sneaks up. We hear visitors as they drive up the tree-lined lane and crunch the gravel on the circle drive. So the knock on the door was not a surprise. But the visitor was — well, sort of.

Uncle Bill was not a real blood uncle, but had been part of the family even before I was born. My father's best friend from the time he was eighteen. His hunting, fishing, drinking, confiding best friend. The man who wrote the eulogy for Dad's funeral. Dad had been gone ten years and Uncle Bill was still dropping in to visit Mom. That was nice. Though my mind flashed briefly back to when I was twelve or thirteen when it wasn't so nice.

Uncle Bill had visited Mom while Dad was working days at the motors. Dad blew up when he found out.

'He knew I was on days. What was he doing here?'

'He's having problems with his marriage. You know what Evelyn is like. He needed someone to talk to.'

After a strained couple of months, Dad and Uncle Bill went back to hunting, fishing, drinking and confiding.

I squeezed Bill's hand in greeting and led him into the living room. He sat in Dad's chair, facing Mom and me sitting on the couch. He'd just returned from a hunting trip with a group of friends — five days, north of North Bay, staying in a hunting lodge. 'They're young guys,' he explained, 'Not an old man like me.'

Uncle Bill was slight, 3 inches shorter than Dad had been, and about two years younger. Though pleasant looking, he didn't match Dad's movie star looks. But Uncle Bill and my father had called each other 'Brother.'

I watched Uncle Bill, this man I'd known all my life, a man I'd grown to love. I hadn't realized he'd stayed friends with Mom, but it seemed natural he'd keep this connection with his best friend's widow, a woman he'd known for over 60 years.

He wouldn't take tea. He had to go. I walked him to the door, grasped his hand in farewell and watched him walk to his pick-up truck. Wondered what he and my mother would have talked about had I not been there.

Mom looked up when I returned to the living room. 'How did Bill look to you?'

'Good,' I responded. 'He looks good.'

'Yes, I think so too,' she replied.

I walked into the kitchen to make her a tuna sandwich for lunch, put it on the coffee table beside her and sat down again in Dad's chair. 'You know I'm flying back home tomorrow.'

'Yes, and I'm not looking forward to you going.'

For the first time, I realized that my independent, outspoken mother was nervous, even fearful, about being on her own.

❊

Four weeks later I flew back again. After Mom had suffered several falls, we, her children, decided she needed full-time care. I had to pack a bag for my mother to take to the nursing home.

I went through her drawers to pick out the things she would need — clothes for comfort, easy to get on and off in case of accidents. Lastly, I opened her underwear drawer. I pushed through utilitarian bras, half-slips, and waist-high white panties in my search for what she'd need. The cream ones? Just white? Then I uncovered some colour, some lace. Red lace. My mother? A flesh-coloured teddy appeared. My mother is in her eighties! Then something rustled at the back of the drawer. A small paper bag. I knew I was snooping, but I had to see what this was, hidden under heaps of underwear. I peeked inside the bag, then reached in and pulled out a small flat box. Inside was a blister pack of pills — medium-blue diamond-shaped pills. Viagra. Viagra in my mother's underwear drawer. I turned over the small box and read the name. W.R. Watson. Uncle Bill.

Uncle Bill? I looked again at the label, just to make sure. Uncle Bill. The prescription had been filled about eighteen months before. Five of the pills were missing. My mother and my dad's best friend. In their eighties. I pushed the box back into the pharmacy bag, hid it in my suitcase and continued packing. I didn't want my sister or brother to find it.

Dad was gone but Uncle Bill was still married to Evelyn, a woman my mother had never liked. If five pills were gone … I tried to block out the images, the thoughts, the teddy. The red lace.

My mother was never a beauty, and she suffered for that. She jealously compared herself with other women she deemed more attractive — including her daughters and her sister. But my mother had an eye for quality, and chose her clothes, bags and shoes carefully. She invested in creams and lotions, make-up and nail polish, had her hair professionally done, and kept herself fit with exercise. Her colour palette never varied from shades of beige and brown, only breaking the monochromatic look with an occasional silk scarf of pale turquoise or green. Tiny earrings and a bracelet of gold completed all outfits. 'Nice' and conservative was the look she strove for.

Mom had complained about my father throughout their marriage. She'd felt unappreciated and criticized by my quiet, nervous, intelligent father who only quit the booze in his late fifties. Both Mom and Dad were loners, and I knew their efforts to bridge the gap between them had been difficult. I suspected she'd had children because that's what women did in the 1950s. She did her duty to us, her children, and to my father, especially when he was dying.

And she'd reached out to someone else. Perhaps Uncle Bill was able to see her sensitive side and appreciate it in a way my father never could.

My mother — controlled, deceptive, judgmental, sharp-tongued, distant. Now she was humbled by illness, no longer in charge of her underwear drawer, her red lace, her teddy, her lover, or her lover's Viagra.

My mother and my father's best friend. Had my father suspected? Had their passion waited, only to flame in earnest after his passing?

I couldn't ask her. I am her daughter, not her confidant. She might lie or, more likely, lash out in anger at such a suggestion. Confused by the chemo or the effects of the cancer, she might just not remember.

But her question, 'How does Bill look to you?' now took on greater significance. In her weakness, she wanted to know, to be reassured. Was he all right?

I couldn't ask my mother anything about this, but decided I would ask Uncle Bill, later, after Mom passed.

If she found the kind of love she wanted in her last years, I will never know. Uncle Bill died of cancer about five months after I last saw him. My mother spent her final days locked in dreams, sitting in her wheelchair, staring silently out the window of her nursing home.

True **friendship** is like sound health; the value of it is seldom known until it is lost.

**CHARLES CALEB COLTON**

# COLLATERAL DAMAGE

## Sue Corke

It was early September 1976, Toronto, Canada. Finally, I had managed to reach Dolores on her home phone. I was anxious to talk to her before she left for the far north.

'I haven't seen you for ages. Let's have coffee when you get back,' I said to her that evening. 'I have something exciting to tell you.'

'No, no, don't keep me hanging, tell me now. I won't be back till next weekend. It takes a whole day to get up there, and then we have the interviews. I want to know now,' Dolores pushed, sensing juicy gossip, but I stayed firm.

'Not now. I want to see your reaction. Safe travels, get some good stories.'

'I'll persuade them to tell me their sex lives,' she cackled. She had sex on the brain.

This was the last conversation we ever had. On 11 September 1976 she died. I didn't find out until a couple of days later; no one really did. In the wild, almost empty space between Moosonee and Timmins the little plane, carrying ten people, hit the hydro wires and flamed out. Some of those who saw the burning remains thought it was a deliberate flare. Only later did the workers at the nearby dam sound the alarm.

It was a terrible accident. Investigators calculated the impact at around 132,000 volts, according to reports in the community newspaper. There had been complaints that the newer hydro wires were often unmarked, pleas for a commission of inquiry. Some speculated that the pilot had been pressured to fly in unsafe conditions in order to get the passengers home for the long weekend ahead. On board were government VIPs and advisors of the Porter Commission on Electrical Supply.

The formal funeral was held in Timmins for politicians and other dignitaries. No one told us about it. Dolores was not a government employee. She had been retained to gauge the community and environmental impact of potential future hydro expansion.

The man who broke the news to me, who hugged me and comforted me that awful day, was my fiancé. We were expecting a baby. That was my big news. My friend would have loved it. She followed my love life with great interest.

'Who's that with the crazy black hair and the honking great laugh?' I whispered to my boss, as the new girl came into the church basement for the first time. She was laughing and joking with the handyman. He was a draft dodger, a good-looking kid. She was already flirting.

'That's our new hire, Dolores,' my boss Eva told me with a grin. Eva was a sweetheart, the chair of the local ratepayers' association. She was the one who had obtained the funding for our local community project.

'What will she do? Where will she sit?' I asked, looking around at that bleak basement space where we operated our little community information centre. We were grateful to the church that lent us the space, but it was spartan.

'She's going to survey seniors in the neighbourhood and find out what they need, then write a report for the Feds.'

It was 1973. I had been in Canada only a few months. I was waiting for my work permit to come through, and was allowed to support myself in the meantime. Although, really, on $100 a week I was actually quite dependent on my sister and her friends, who allowed me to stay with them rent free.

We were a ragtag little group in that holy basement: Jon, the draft dodger handyman; Terry, the hippie; Dolores, the loud American; and me, the uptight Brit. We were irreverent, noisy and largely ignorant of the information we were hired to share. We averaged four calls a day, and perhaps one walk-in. We had difficulty remembering which services were delivered by which level of government, and our advice was sometimes quite wrong. But we were always there, until nine o'clock at night. Some of our phone-ins were actually misplaced distress calls, so we may have saved a couple of lives to justify our existence. Later the YWCA did an audit of our productivity and of course we were shut down. But that was in 1974. We had a year together and we bonded, Dolores and I. She was uninhibited, hugely funny and a bit naughty. Her legs were so hairy she was ashamed of them, always wore black tailored pants to cover them.

One day in the washroom we shared a secret. We both fancied the draft dodger. It was no contest; she got him.

'What these old girls want are their sex lives back,' Dolores reported, deadpan, one afternoon on her return from a strenuous morning of calling on neighbourhood seniors, drinking their tea and eating their angel cake.

'Pretty sure the government won't respond to that finding,' I countered. Jon said he would be willing and able to help, if there was a program for it.

Dolores had a husband who had been injured in the Vietnam war. They had both come to Canada after his discharge to try to pick up the pieces, but she was starting to give up. He was very different now than when she had married him. He had unpredictable outbursts and dark, dark days. Dolores was getting tired of trying. I was just recently divorced and a bit fragile. We were both young still and looking for love, back then in 1973. We hung out sometimes.

Her friends were older than I was and a bit intimidating. Although she was quite boisterous and had a crude sense of humour, I thought she was very sophisticated. She had a university education, which had eluded me then, came from a well-to-do family and knew a lot of things about the Vietnam war. I fancied myself a peacenik in those days. I was interested in the protest movement in America. She clued me in.

'You're so uptight. Relax a little,' she would tell me. But I was full of anxiety about my new life, my work prospects, what would happen after this little interlude. Laughing with her over silly hilarious things really helped. I remember the day the pastor from the church visited us unexpectedly and found us eating pizza in his Sunday school room, boxes and crusts everywhere. He was a young man, a Christian Scientist, and as he reprimanded us in the name of his god for our disrespectful behaviour, three of us, similar in age to this earnest fellow, tried to apologize. But Dolores instigated a fit of laughter that caught among us till we hid our faces in shame. She explained that God would want us to eat.

❁

When the funding came to an end the handyman sought amnesty and eventually went back to America. I applied as a mature student to the University of Toronto to study community planning. And Dolores got the coveted job as a citizen participation analyst for CELA, the Canadian Environmental Law Association. We stayed in touch. The last time I had dinner at her house it was Halloween. She had brought an armful of bright autumn leaves into their rented house and thrown them all over the floors.

She cooked exotic vegan food. She told rude and crazy stories to the whole room. She was so light.

Just before she died she fell in love with an English guy. She was happy, she said. The way things worked, though, the protocols of death, all the logistics, those arrangements, they didn't include him. It was heartbreaking. It was left to her estranged husband to bury her.

I went with one of the sophisticated American friends to clean out her things to ship back to her mother. It was a solemn and largely silent afternoon. I could not find the words to share my grief. I remember that she had a surprising number of shoes. A song by Chicago always takes me back to that time, even now, four decades later.

I didn't have many friends when I first came to Canada. I took a long time to warm up to people. Dolores wasn't having any of that stand-offish British stuff. She cut right through it. She was a big personality, a lovely friend, a constant surprise. I think it would have been so much fun to have had her around. She would have lightened some of the heaviness of these past 40 years, and deeply enjoyed some of the more insane adventures.

In my more pensive moments I think that she was collateral damage from the Vietnam war. That's the only reason she was in Canada, after all, to put that behind her, to try to give her partner an opportunity to mend. They came for a new start. It just didn't pan out.

When you are hit with life-disrupting events, you will never be the same again. You either cope or you crumble; you become better or bitter; you emerge stronger or weaker.

**AL SIEBERT**

# AFTERMATH

## Margie Taylor

Learning to walk again. That's what it can feel like after you've lost a loved one. The death of a partner, the aftermath of divorce, the loss of a parent or child, a beloved sibling or friend — sometimes the pain is so wrenching it feels as if the normal patterns of life have fallen away.

How did you used to walk? How did it feel to wake up in the morning and have that person in your life? Who will support you now — who will tell you you're going to be okay, you'll get through this, you'll find your way?

You've entered an unknown country. You've arrived there without a guidebook, not speaking the language, not knowing the rules. And you really, really don't want to be there. This new place is familiar and yet different. There are streets, houses, apartment buildings. People commute to work, take their dogs for a walk, shop for groceries, play with their children. The sun rises and sets, it gets cold at night, warms up during the day. The very familiarity is jarring: shouldn't it stop, if only for a moment? How can it be that the world can carry on when the one who made it interesting has gone?

You feel like Alice, viewing the world through a looking glass. An invisible wall separates you from the others. In time, the wall will melt. You, too, will shop and commute and maybe take a few tottering steps in this new place, hoping you won't fall and make a fool of yourself. Maybe you'll join a group or take up a hobby. You'll find a way to stop feeling guilty about being alive — stop apologizing for things you said or should have said.

❁

You never saw yourself as a wife. The word had such baggage — love, honour, obey. Housework. All those things you dismissed when you were young. How could they compete with freedom — adventure — finding yourself? And then you take the plunge and find yourself sharing your life with this other person who likes some of the same things. Greek food. British humour. Sex. The Beatles. Is that enough? There are times when it isn't. Shouldn't there be poetry? Romance? Money?

Oh, yes. Money. It's the only thing you fight about. No, correct that: you fight, he listens. Or goes into the other room. Or stays up late afterwards, watching soccer. While you storm upstairs, slam the door, determined not to cry.

He comes to bed, thinking you're asleep. Hoping it's one of those time-of-the-month things. Which it is, sometimes. But not always.

Why do you go on? Why does he stay? Why do you continue to believe it's worth it? You have your reasons. There was, after all, that time with the sofa.

It was early in the relationship. You'd been together a few weeks — a month, maybe. You were sleeping together of course … well, you weren't kids. He'd been married before, you'd had lovers. You were adults. You went to bed on your first date. Which you, a child of the Sixties, shouldn't have to explain but somehow feel that you do.

So: the sofa. It was an old, green, second-hand couch left behind by your former roommate.

Actually, second-hand is being kind. By the time it came to you it had been through many hands. It had not been treated kindly. There were stains on it that might have been left by incontinent cats but you were inclined to suspect fornicating couples, given the source. It sagged where it shouldn't and bulged in unexpected places. You made a point of putting a towel down when you sat on it. When your roommate moved out you insisted he take it with him. It had come from his friends after all, not yours. He refused, said it wouldn't fit in his new place. His one concession was to drag it out of the living room into the bedroom. And now every morning when you opened your eyes there it was, leering at you, a great green blister waiting to erupt.

You tried to sell it with no luck. You couldn't even give it away. Goodwill came and took a look and said they didn't want it. The Salvation Army wouldn't even come and see it. Nobody at work was interested. It wasn't old enough to be interesting or new enough to be desirable. It was just an old couch.

It was Saturday. You and he were in bed, thinking about getting up and heading out for coffee and a paper. The sun streamed in through the bedroom window. The sofa, if possible, looked even worse in the daylight.

'God, I hate that couch.'

'What's the matter with it?'

'Everything.'

'It doesn't look so bad to me. Why do you hate it?'

And so you told him. You'd told others about that couch. You'd mentioned it at work a dozen times, whined about it to friends, considered paying someone to take it to the dump. If you knew someone with a truck. Who was strong enough to lug it downstairs — there was no elevator. Who was willing to take the time to do it.

People were sympathetic. They made suggestions: have you called Goodwill? Yes. Maybe you should put a notice in the grocery store. Tried that, they took it down. Is it worth getting it reupholstered? It could be fine with a new cover. No, it couldn't. Try ignoring it. I can't.

Now you said it was more than just a piece of furniture. That couch, you said, represented everything you loathed about your ex-roommate. Not being able to make it disappear made you feel helpless. You did not want to live your life with your ex-roommate's castoffs.

He got up, got dressed, said he'd be back in half an hour. When he came back he had a saw and a hammer. He sawed the couch into three pieces, carried each section to the second-storey balcony and dropped it on the pavement below. Then he went downstairs, picked up the sections and carried them around the back to the dumpster. The couch was gone. He made it disappear.

That was it. That was when you knew. This was a man who could make things go away. Who would chop a couch in half — in three pieces, actually — simply because it bothered you.

A few weeks ago you made a wrong turn and drove past your old apartment. You thought of the sofa. The balcony is still there — the dumpster may be gone. It would be harder now to get rid of an old couch. But he'd find a way.

❄

Eventually, you will stop envying those on the other side of the wall. The ones who haven't experienced this kind of loss. The ones who can still take the present for granted, as you used to do, and assume the future will continue. Your own future has changed forever. At some point, you'll see the way forward. You'll find a way to navigate the trails in this part of the world.

Right now, though, if you could, you'd go back in time — not far back, just far enough. Back to when you took for granted all the bits and pieces that make up a day. The small conversations, the shared jokes, even the occasional arguments. In this strange new country the stories aren't remembered … they're waiting to be told.

Folks are usually about
as happy as they make
their minds up to be.

**ABRAHAM LINCOLN**

# BUT NOT FOR ME

## Roger Chapman

The salesman thinks I'm a shrimp. I can tell by his ever-so-slightly sneering tone, when he says to my mother, 'Don't worry, madam, he'll grow into it. It should last him for years.'

We're in Daniel Neal, the West End children's department store, and he's talking about my just-bought dressing gown, a gaudy affair in red, green and orange towelling, large enough for a seven-year-old shrimp to use as a tent. I'm not really interested in what the salesman thinks or, for that matter, the dressing gown. No — I'm much more focused on the real, yet-to-come highlight of the day: lunch in a restaurant. I don't even mind having to grope through the winter fog to get there.

The restaurant is unspeakably posh. Waiters, tailcoated and aproned, stride to and fro across the room, trays balanced on upturned fingers. I know it's rude to stare, so I try not to make it too obvious, looking up surreptitiously from my plate as often as I dare.

Time for pudding. 'What would you like?' says Mother. 'You can have roly poly pudding, or treacle tart, or bread and butter pudding.'

Treacle tart is my favourite, but roly poly pudding is a close second.

Such a difficult decision needs a lot of thought, and it may take me a while.

Before I have a chance to consider it, I notice another waiter — an obviously superior person — marching towards the next table with purpose written over his face and his nose in the air. Even his moustache seems to stand to attention.

Yet it's not how he looks but what he's carrying that transfixes me — a stupendously tall glass filled to overflowing with a tower of ice-cream, fruit, jelly, cream, syrup, nuts, hundreds and thousands, or sprinkles, and who knows what else. I can't take my eyes off it (though a corner of my mind also thinks what a terrible waste of ice-cream it would be if he tripped). After this, even treacle tart would be a let-down.

'What's that, Mum?'

'It's a Knickerbocker Glory, dear.'

'Can I have one? Please.'

But Mother says no. Because I'm so short, I'd have to stand on my chair to eat it, wielding a spoon long enough to reach the bottom of the glass. This would draw attention to me in an un-British way (as if I care), and we can't be having that. I don't feel convinced, and I suspect she's just made it up. I protest, but it makes no difference. My consolation prize is that I'm allowed strawberry ice-cream 'as a special treat'. Any other day I'd be excited about that, but now it tastes of disappointment.

❀

Tonight, we've arranged to meet our friends Gordon and Hilary for dinner and a concert. Gordon, a man who knows a thing or two about eating out, has chosen the restaurant, which, he says, has been well reviewed.

The first thing I notice when we reach our table is the array of huge, pretentious wine glasses which stand teetering on impossibly long stems, looking as if they might topple over at any moment. Holding one while you drink from it is a gymnastic feat in itself. Only a little larger and you could probably have a bath in it. We order wine while we're discussing the menu.

The waiter returns with the bottle already open and empties it into four of the glasses, creating not much more than a puddle in the bottom of each. She then enquires if we want another bottle — an invitation we have no difficulty in refusing.

Time now to look at the menu. I've just read a book that explains how to tell an expensive restaurant from the narrations on the menu, without even looking at the prices, so I intend to put this to the test. From the very first item — 'Our very own whitebait, fresh from the West Coast, served in a light but elegant batter with a hint of lemon' — I realize immediately that it's my wallet which is in for a battering. Eventually I shrug and settle for the deeply suspicious 'Succulent suprême of corn-fed chicken, with our chef's special mushroom cream sauce made to his secret recipe, enhanced by freshly dug buttered new potatoes and local garden peas', even though the chef's secret is probably that he found the recipe in someone else's cookbook.

Before closing the menu, I peek at the dessert list and find that it includes Knickerbocker Glory. I avoid reading any further, for fear of coming upon another overblown description. Sixty and a few years after I wasn't allowed one, I'm still to eat a Knickerbocker Glory — though the pangs of deprivation are less intense now. I've never even seen one listed on a menu. I suppose I could have made my own at any time, but where's the fun in that? Surely much of the pleasure of having a KG is in ordering it, and then watching it approach you across the room. And there's the half-felt fear that what I remember has been enlarged by the magnifying lens of age, that it won't live up to the image of what I saw all those years ago.

But now, at last, I have another chance — if I don't have a starter, there'll be time for dessert. As the waiter departs for the kitchen, Gordon tells her that we must leave by 7.30 for our concert. She says that she will inform the chef.

We chatter among ourselves and try the wine. Time passes. We try the wine again. When the waiter comes once more within hailing distance, Gordon reminds her of our deadline and asks politely when the food is likely to arrive.

After what we assume is a sortie to the kitchen, she returns to tell us brightly that it will be ready in a few minutes.

Time passes. When almost all the wine has been drunk, the food shows up. Or, to be precise, three-quarters of it. My dinner is nowhere in sight. I alone have been singled out for special treatment. While the others face appetizing and well-filled plates, I am confronted by nothing more substantial than the tablecloth.

Ridiculously, I feel slightly embarrassed, but my meal will surely arrive at any moment, and I encourage the others to begin.

Time passes. Nothing happens, beyond the sounds of eating and Hilary making sympathetic noises. The waiter fails to notice any problem, but then she comes within eye-shot and I ask where my order is. She looks no more than mildly surprised and says that she will check with the chef.

Time passes. The waiter reappears and tells me without the slightest hint of an apology that my meal is 'just coming', as if this kind of staggered — not to say haphazard — service is normal.

When my food finally makes its entrance, the others have almost finished theirs. I'll have to eat quickly so as not to keep them waiting. And, slightly to my surprise, it does look pretty succulent. But that's the end of the good news. The first mouthful is no more than tepid. And when I begin to dissect the chicken, the inside proves to be a vivid pink. In the ordinary way, I might have sighed, pushed the chicken to one side, and carried on eating the remaining contents of my plate. While this is tempting, I'm now feeling sufficiently annoyed to complain. Just at this moment, the waiter materializes and asks, in a voice which indicates that she has no interest in the response, if everything is alright. I grab my opportunity.

'I'm sorry, but my food is cold.' I'm not sure why I'm the one apologizing. 'And this chicken isn't cooked.'

'No, sir — it is cooked. The chef normally serves it medium–rare.'

If this chicken was any pinker, it would still be clucking. But with extreme self-restraint, I say, 'That's hard to believe. Surely the chef knows how dangerous undercooked chicken is. Anyway, I'd like mine properly cooked, so please take this away.'

The lips compress. 'Well, sir –', she begins. But before she can resume the debate, the maître d' shimmers up to our table, spies the carnage on my plate, apologizes and removes it. I'm not certain how much longer I may have to wait for any edible dinner, but matters are about to be taken out of my hands.

Gordon looks pointedly at his watch. 'We have to go in a couple of minutes.' The waiter is still hovering. I ask how long it's going to take to finish cooking my meal, but I can already guess the answer: 'I'll just check with the chef.'

While I'm buttoning my coat, another waiter passes by. He's carrying a tall glass filled to overflowing with a tower of ice-cream, fruit, jelly, cream, syrup, nuts, hundreds and thousands, and who knows what else.

We remember
their love,
when they
can no longer
remember.

UNKNOWN

# WHO KNOWS?

## Tania Park

So still you sat there staring into the unknown. A look of stunned bewilderment on your face made your eyes appear to be more hollow than usual. From my position on the end of the pew I wondered if you knew what was going on. A continuous scuffle of creeping shoes and hushed whispers of mourners made more noise than they wanted to in their attempts to show the deference the solemn occasion deserved. The sibilant sounds echoing from hard surfaces seemed to rebound from the soaring domed ceiling, giving an even eerier atmosphere than the crematorium already possessed.

As you stared straight ahead I followed your line of sight until my eyes rested on the polished pine coffin. My heart hitched as I slid my eyelids shut for a moment of reflection.

Did you know who was resting inside?

You looked so pretty with your permed curls coiffed with such care. Someone had made sure you looked your best. The pure white hair gave away your age but the softness of almost wrinkle-free skin on your face belied your 82 years. Your daily ritual of moisturizer all your life had paid dividends. Pink had always been your favourite colour and, thankfully, that same someone had dressed you in the softest shades, giving your cheeks a rosy glow. If ever there was a typical peaches and cream complexion, then you had it.

Almost as if you were reading my mind, you twisted your head and glanced at me then reached out one time-wrinkled but still graceful hand. How clever those hands had been. A skilled dressmaker, you used those hands to create the most amazing outfits for so many years. Wedding gowns, shirts, dresses, tutus and ballet costumes all flew from those agile fingers, delighting the wearers: especially me. The cooking. Oh, wow!

You weren't satisfied with winning one blue ribbon for the most outstanding cook at the Royal Show. No, you had to do it again and then again. Lucky us were given what you regarded as the not-so-perfect results.

Then there was the art, of so many genres. Amazing prize-winning pieces in oils, watercolours, china painting, printmaking, enamelling and silverwork all came from those hands. Heartbreaking was the day you were given basic tests and asked to draw a triangle. A 10-tonne block of concrete pressed into my chest when you fumbled with a simple pencil trying to figure out what it was and what the hell to do with it. A simple triangle was beyond you. Scrawling the scribble of an infant's first attempt with a crayon was all you could achieve. Your attempt broke something inside me.

Moisture glimmered on the edge of your creamy lashes as I grasped your cold hand and wrapped my equally frigid fingers around yours to give you the warmth of a touch you seemed to be seeking. I wondered if the tears were because you had realized it was a funeral or maybe you really did know who was resting in that box. You slid across the polished wood to get closer. Joy burst inside me and warmed my heart. You knew who I was. You wanted a hug.

'Who are you?' you whispered.

I tried not to let it hurt.

The tears vanished and a smile shot out the moment the music began. Every single word of the 23rd psalm tripped from your tongue along with everyone else. Somewhere in that vacant mind the music was still there, and you didn't care who I was. For the few minutes of the song you were happy and aware.

I was the only one of your children you regularly recognized. I will never know if that recognition was through that special mother–daughter bond. But this day I wasn't sure if you even knew me. No recognition shone from your eyes each time you peeked at me during the service.

For years now your mind had gradually disintegrated to the extent that every time I visited, you took me aside with a concerned frown and asked me to get rid of the strange men wandering around the house. That the men in question were your husband of 60 years and your 50-year-old son who was now your carer, didn't ease your concern. Even after having a special afternoon tea and introducing your husband to you, you still didn't recognize him. We pointed to the worn wedding ring on your finger and explained that the elderly man next to you was the husband you had devoted your life to caring for. But you wouldn't accept that. To you he was a complete stranger invading your home. Your husband was the curly-headed young man in the wedding photo on the mantle. Not this white-headed octogenarian with a large bald patch.

We stood to attention in sombre silence as the coffin lowered into that mysterious, spooky void under the floor, my arm around your shoulder. Tears poured unchecked down my cheeks at the simple action of you stooping to kiss the coffin of the trespassing stranger. For a brief moment I think you knew, for I'm sure I heard a whispered, 'Goodbye, Bob'. But ten minutes later, while partaking of afternoon tea, your eyes were as vacant as your mind and I couldn't help but think that maybe you really didn't have a clue.

❄

Less than a month later I had my answer. Wearing pink, as were all the mourners as you despised black and had never worn a skerrick of the colour in your life, tears welled behind my dark glasses as I stood alongside your four sons in the searing heat of the midday summer sun. With our hearts lodged somewhere really uncomfortable we watched a similar casket, but this time in jarrah, being lowered into the ground. How scarily weird it was that a mind-deprived woman who otherwise had no health problems had gone downhill with such rapidity. It was as though life had been sucked from you.

I wasn't given a chance to say goodbye. Even if you were unable to recognize or fathom the passing of your husband, one of those mysteries of life that scientists still had no logical answers for, had drawn you to spend eternity with your life partner.

Your soul knew.

I can wipe away the tears from my eyes. But … I can't wipe away the pain in my heart.

UNKNOWN

# A LONG WAIT

## Margaret Callow

Every few months a small group of women meet. Never in each other's houses, but in a dingy room above a church hall that smells of faded polish and ageing furniture. One thing unites them. A dreadful pain that lasts decades. No one told them long years would pass when they wrestled with their sense of loss. That heartache and guilt would become their secret companions. Unmarried motherhood a cause of shame and disgrace. Social revolution has yet to come. Forty-plus years and they are still haunted.

❄

Enemy bombing appeared to be at an end, the May skies above London quiet, and on the ground, less fearful, folk moved freely again.

'But that's wonderful, Rose.' The words were muttered and joyless. 'There's no mistake? You are sure?'

She nodded, anxious to read Henry's face. His expression told her all she needed to know.

'I'm sorry. Are you angry?'

'No, not angry, my darling girl. It's just there is so much to consider. My finals, the hospital and then there is the war. Father is very keen I join up once I've qualified, in the navy like him.'

Unable to find the right words, any words in fact, Rose gnawed her lip.

'Oh God, Rose, what are we to do?' he said. 'You do know I can't marry you? I have no money of my own, only the allowance my parents give me. I had thought when the war was over, if we still felt the same, well, then we might ...' He rubbed his forehead in an impatient gesture. His words trailed away and his shoulders were hunched in misery. Rose fought to control her distress. They walked towards the hospital in silence, each wrapped in their own thoughts. At the door of the nurses' home, he said, 'People mustn't know. How long can you work? I shall have to tell the parents, perhaps you could stay with them.'

'As you wish, Henry.'

Her words sounded forlorn, his were jumbled like his thoughts. A brief kiss and he strode off towards the medical school. He didn't look back. She could barely see him through a haze of tears.

Marjorie Mason towered over Rose. Pale cheeked, lips pinched, eyes narrowed and devoid of any warmth, she hissed her anger. 'You stupid child. So you thought this would catch my son. But you are a nothing, a nobody, and I will not allow you to ruin his future. He will qualify soon and like all the men in the family he will make a name for himself as a brilliant surgeon in one of London's great hospitals. If he persists in this liaison with you, we shall cut him off without a penny. There will be no bastard welcomed into this family.'

Rose slumped lower into the faded floral covers of a wing-backed chair, one of a pair in front of the austere fireplace. Despite the warmth flooding through the open French doors, she shivered as if the ague nipped at her bones. Marjorie looked down at her with a dispassionate stare before she moved away. Looking faraway into the distance, she sucked in her breath and then said briskly, 'The arrangements have all been made. The moment Henry told us, I knew what must be done and there is no time to waste. You will leave the hospital, tell them anything you like except of course the truth. There must be no word of this outside this house. Is that understood?'

It was a struggle for Rose to speak, her tongue seemed too large in her mouth and her throat felt so dry each word rasped against soft flesh.

'Yes, yes,' she mumbled finally.

Marjorie nodded. 'Henry tells us the birth is due at the end of November so you will take a room with us and then before the time, you will travel to Devon. There is a home for unmarried mothers and they will have a bed for you. I'm told it is clean and quite comfortable. You will stay there to have the child and then two weeks after the birth, you will give it up for adoption. Is that clear?'

Rosie's pain behaved like spilt acid, spreading across her features, dissolving her soft skin, casting shadows across her large, dark eyes and melting her full lips and ready smile. It seemed an age before she could articulate her words and when she did, her voice sounded tiny. 'No. Please, please, I want my baby. It is Henry's and mine, our baby. I want our child.'

'You are not in a position to want anything, my dear, and that is that.'

Marjorie crossed the room in a long stride and pushed the small button bell set beside the marble fire surround. In abject misery, Rose watched her. Henry's mother was right, of course; she was indeed powerless to alter things, but any hopes she might have had for understanding soon shrivelled away, too.

'We'll take tea now, Doris,' Marjorie said, with a sweet smile.

She waited until the door closed again, before beckoning into the garden in order to summon Henry and his father. 'Tea,' she trilled.

The tray shone with silver polish and with every movement, the glass beads on the milk jug cover tinkled against delicate bone china. Doris knew exactly where to set the tea down and a with a bob of her head, left the room again.

Marjorie nodded at the plate of freshly made scones, 'So fortunate we don't have to bother much with rationing. Does your family find things difficult, Rose?'

'I told you, Mother, Rose lives in the nurses' home,' Henry said.

'Did you, dear? I really can't recall.'

Neville Mason's hawkish eyes behind steel-rimmed glasses seemed reluctant to settle on Rose, rather more to concentrate on the crumbs left on his tea plate. Finally he leaned back to be comfortable in his chair and cleared his throat. 'Everything sorted now?' he said to no one in particular.

It seemed only Marjorie could answer. Henry's lips were tight, his expression one of gloom and Rose sat fighting back the tears.

'Perfectly, dear,' she said. 'I have explained to Rose how regrettable events are, but she understands Henry has an important time ahead of him and nothing must interfere with that.'

'That's it, that's it exactly,' Neville boomed. 'We expect great things from you, my boy, and this is no time to be bogged down by …' His words trailed away, leaving an awkward silence.

'The pair of you have just been rather silly, that's all. There is nothing for you to worry about, so do cheer up,' Marjorie enthused. 'This sort of thing happens all the time, so I'm told, adoption that is. All very private and no one ever need know. Arrangements are made behind closed doors, as they say, and the people who handle it are very careful.'

'Very careful, I'm sure,' Neville echoed.

'Something wrong with your tea, Rose dear?' Marjorie enquired, her hand gesture indicating the full cup standing on a small, highly polished mahogany table, one of a nest of three.

❧

It would come without warning — she could be walking in a park, shopping in a supermarket, doing the housework and suddenly the memory was there, especially on birthdays. There was a time when more than half a million women knew the trauma of giving their newborn child to someone else under pressure and Rose was one of them. Knowledge that she could love yet never know her baby marred her life.

Now the passing years, like age, have brought wisdom — a new openness, an understanding of love lost and an end to such anguish. I know of these things because I am Rose and Henry's child.

Sometimes you will never know the value of a moment until it becomes a memory.

**DR SEUSS**

# THE SWORD DANCE

## Susan Braghieri

There is the memory; my only memory of him. The kitchen tiles are cold under my bare feet. Alternating squares of grey and black, grey and black. I look through to the living room. My father is sitting on the sofa with my baby brother, Michael, perched on his knee. I move through the doorway onto the timber floorboards. They feel smooth. I call Michael's name.

He turns his head to my voice, and my body starts to move. I lift one arm above my head, with the other bent on my hip. I kick my legs like the dancers I've seen on TV; the ones who perform for the Queen in their tartan skirts and socks. I pretend there are two swords on the floor and I dance around them. The bagpipe music is playing in my head. Michael starts to laugh. It's a gurgle of delight. He giggles and giggles, Dad bouncing him in time to each laugh. I finish my dance. My father holds Michael's hands and claps them together. I take a bow.

I don't ever want to lose this moment, this enduring memory of Michael. The only one of my siblings to have black curly hair and the genetic gift of blue eyes. It's the one time I can remember his face. I often wondered how old I was at the time, but recall it was before I started school. My mother, however, was always somewhat vague about this.

'Oh, probably around four or so, or maybe three and a half,' she'd say, any time I asked. The conversation over before it started.

I remember trips to the local cemetery on the other side of town when I was in primary school. The cemetery located amidst drought-ridden paddocks, and surrounded by barbed wire fencing to keep out the neighbouring farmer's cattle. The graves were clustered at the top end of the cemetery lot, with an expanse of brittle grass on the lower end where visitors parked their cars. I remember the weeds and spear grass sprouting beside the neglected headstones of the old graves, the ageing grey cement collapsing in places. I recall wandering up and down the rows inventing stories for the people who were buried there, while my parents tended to our baby brothers' grave. There was a sadness in seeing tombstones for other babies and young children, and I'd wonder why they had died.

Our family grave was in the newer section. A modest, rendered concrete grave with a geometric pattern on top, and painted in pale blue with a white border. The names of my baby brothers, Michael and Timothy, were inscribed on their headstone along with their ages. I never got to see my other baby brother, Timothy, who was born after Michael. He was a complete mystery to me. He was born too early, my mother later told me, and never came home, dying within an hour of his birth. A simple explanation to silence the curiosity of a sister, still a child herself and far too young to understand the complexities of what that really meant. My two baby brothers dying within months of each other, so they were buried together.

I don't remember anything about their passing. It's not surprising. I now know they died in the months leading up to my fourth birthday — the dates of their deaths discovered in online records. There must have been a hush over our house, a weight of silence and sorrow that enveloped everything. And I don't recall going to their funerals; a rite that children were often kept away from in those days. My siblings and I may well have gone, but I have no memory of it. The enormity of the grief.

I asked my mother about Michael over the years when I was older, a teenager and, later, a woman with babies of my own. Old enough to hear why Michael never made it to his first birthday, and mature enough to know that things can go silently wrong while a baby is growing in your belly. Bit by bit, my mother relinquished more information.

My parents took Michael to see a specialist at a children's hospital in the city to find out why he wasn't meeting his milestones. They waited days for the specialist to see him, and when they were allowed to visit, they'd arrive to find other sick children climbing in and out of his cot. When the doctor didn't find anything obvious wrong with him, Michael was discharged. He became ill on his return home and died in our local hospital from complications from pneumonia, an autopsy revealing my baby brother had a hole in his heart. The pneumonia too much for his ailing body. My mother shared her despair that a surgical cure for his heart condition was developed only a few years later. There are all the unspoken 'what ifs', the musings I allow my mind to take thinking about the life that could have been ours with him in it, instead of the space of his absence. I find myself yearning for more remembrances of Michael, memories like those I have of my own sons when they were babies. Tactile moments: the softness of his skin, the brush of his black curls against my cheek, and the touch of his tiny fingers as they curled around mine. I want to remember his scent when he was clean and fresh after a bath and dusted with baby powder, but most of all I want to recall those blue eyes looking into mine. But I have no such moments to cherish. Only my sword dance.

I wonder sometimes, too, if I have imagined the memory of dancing for Michael. My recollections of myself at that age are scant, and more tellingly, we have no photos of him. Is this a phantom memory that I think I remember? Did my parents, or siblings, tell me about it and I have adopted it as my own? But I dismiss this. I can feel it in my limbs; the movement of the dance in my arms and legs. I hear again his laugh. I've never forgotten his laugh. No, there is no doubt in my mind. My body remembers.

When the **sun has set,** no candle can replace it.

**GEORGE R.R. MARTIN**

# THE TWO OF US

## Anne Jenner

I visit her now three times a week: Monday afternoons, Wednesday mornings, Friday afternoons. I've been told a fixed schedule is better for her. Not because it gives her something to look forward to. Her ability to anticipate future events, let alone put a date to them, has vanished. It's to do with the need to vary her day. I was told this by a nurse with a Scottish accent so broad I thought at first she said 'value'. Variety or value, both good reasons, so I go along with it happily. Although there was a time when Mum would have argued, vehemently, for spontaneity over structure.

But this is now. And so at the ages of 64 and 86 respectively, we're spending more time together, just the two of us, than ever before. Over the years our intimacy has always been compromised by others with competing needs — siblings, spouses, children — a long line of stepping stones between two very divergent paths. And I, at least, preferred it that way. Distance was what I craved. As I grew older, separation from her became my goal. 'I am not my mother' was the silent mantra that guided my increasingly daring expeditions into worlds she'd never dared venture.

When I was little I asked her questions all the time, unanswerable ones like how far up is the sky? But later that stopped. Because I thought I had all the answers, or I assumed hers would be hopelessly inappropriate. Now, as a mother myself,

I know the gratification of being asked. For anything, even my recipe for tiramisu. People talk about the arrogance of youth, but it's more a case of flawed peripheral vision.

You can't see beyond the circumscribed landscape of your own bubble. Now the questions I ask her are different, both elemental and consequential at the same time. Who am I? Where are you? What day is it? What did you have for lunch? Some days she doesn't know the answer to any of them. Her eyes are watery again. Blocked tear ducts. I open my bag to find a clean tissue. My phone falls out. 'What's that?' she asks, eyeing it warily. We gave her one once, pre-programmed with my number, my husband's, the doctor's and her neighbour's. It soon became clear that was too many and we cut it down to mine only. Until that became superfluous.

'Don't you remember?' I ask. It's good, apparently, to prevaricate a bit. Don't answer straightaway. Challenge the cognitive process. But it rarely works. The eyes go blank, as if a blind's been drawn on a room that's not used any more. All the furniture, those elegant shining pieces covered now in dust sheets.

She's lost more weight. Her nightgown gapes at the neck. It keeps slipping off one or the other emaciated shoulder, a parody of coquettishness that makes her look vulnerable. I make a note to get her some new nightgowns. Ted would say it's a waste. She's not going to be around much longer. It's not because he says things like this that we're separated. But it's contributed. You can go on inwardly recoiling from attitudes you find repellent for a long time. And I have. It's when you look across the table one day and know not only has the use-by date expired, but the thing's turned rancid, that you have to stop.

Mum doesn't know about the separation. From the moment Ted became a fixture in my life, she doted on him. They played little flirty games as if she was his girl, not me.

'How's the lovely Belinda,' he'd say and she'd giggle and pat him playfully on the arm. Even through the 30-odd years of our marriage and two children, they kept their special bond. 'How's Ted?' usually superseded 'How are you?' in our phone calls. Is it her I'm trying to protect by keeping it quiet? Or him? How, in any case, to explain a ruptured marriage to someone whose brain is coagulating under an accumulation far more caustic than hurtful words.

She hasn't mentioned Ted for a while. He hasn't been to see her since he left so maybe she's forgotten him. Although her memory's erratic, one day telling me a story about a long-ago local minister who ran off with the daughter of one of his parishioners, other days asking if Ralph is coming soon. Ralph is my father who died seven years ago. A sudden heart attack. Ted says it's a good thing he didn't live to see his wife lose her mind.

Her room is clammy, blanketed in the cloying smell of stale talc, roses wilting in brackish water along the windowsill, institutional cooking and something else, the chalky smell of age. We used to joke about her refined sense of smell, her addiction to fragrance, the herbs hung in her kitchen, the scented sachets in every drawer, the aromatic diffusers in every room. She explained it as hypertrophied olfactory glands, a term she picked up from her obsessive reading of medical journals. 'I should have been a doctor,' she used to say. 'I love the way they order and classify everything. Making a diagnosis must be so satisfying, like solving a puzzle.' When I asked her once why she hadn't followed her love of science and chosen it as a profession, she gazed off into the middle distance as if trying to re-enter her younger self, then shrugged and said it was a different time back then.

The squeak of rubber soled shoes in the corridor. A nurse puts her head around the door. She looks about fourteen. 'Would you like those put in water?' she asks, with a nod towards the untidy clump of pink camellias throttled in foil on the bedside table.

'What's that dear?' Mum asks, her forehead crinkling in a frown.

'The nurse is getting some water for the flowers.'

'No, no, I don't want water. They put something in it, you know.' A pink tide rises up her neck and her knotty fingers pluck agitatedly at the counterpane.

'Don't worry,' I tell the nurse. 'I'll do it.' At one time I'd be led by these fretful episodes into rescue attempts. I'd reassure her there's no conspiracy, no perpetrators of evil intent on harm but all it did was make it worse. Acknowledgment of whatever restless waves break on the shoreline of her rock-strewn consciousness is tantamount to admission of the threat, so now I don't buy in.

Outside the window there's a garden, manicured into submission daily by an Indian man with a thick black moustache. I look out at a row of rose bushes neatly pruned, ranged along a mound of mulched earth. Eruptions of tiny leaves and nodules crown the spiky stems, nascent blooms that will in a few weeks' time unfold and hold their faces to the sun.

On the days my mother is allowed up I'll wheel her chair over to the glass and point this out to her, the seasonal resurrection.

A year or so ago, she stuck a post-it note on the inside of her back door that said 'back garden' and one on the front door that said 'exit'. When I asked about them she said it was so she wouldn't get lost. That was when we decided living alone was no longer an option.

Leaving is always my undoing. I bend down, put my lips to her tissue paper skin, fold my hand around the white knuckled trembling of hers. I smile at her serenely while love and loss and the craving for escape fight their internecine war in my heart.

'I'm going now Mum,' I say, smoothing her hair where it's bushed up at the back of her head. Her miraculous hair, the one thing of hers I wished I'd inherited. Thick and springy, fading as she aged into that mellow silvery ash that it would have been a crime to colour. Mine comes from Dad. Fine and fly-away, masquerading now as a honey brown that gives itself away every four weeks to dishrag grey at the crown and temples.

'Wait a minute,' she says just before I turn away. Her eyes are locked on mine. 'Has Ted gone?' Her hand grasps my wrist, tightens. I can't pull away, either from the question or her grip. Just like when I was small and she'd found me out in a fib. And just like then, my face colours, my tongue flounders, words won't come.

'Ted. Your husband,' she says crisply. 'Don't you think I know who he is?'

'Oh, Mum.' I sigh and wipe my hand across my forehead. I sit down again, my legs shaky. She relaxes her grip and her soft old fingers flutter against my hand. And I see she's smiling at me, her eyes lit from within, as though from the brief flare of a match.

'It's alright dear,' she says. 'I know. You deserve better.'

Count your age by **friends**, not years. Count your life by smiles, not **tears**.

**JOHN LENNON**

# SMALL THINGS

## Marion Day

It's the small things I remember.

My father's bulbous stomach, which pushed high into his ribcage making it difficult to breathe, so he never sat upright, but had to lean over tables, bum always on the edge of the chair. The scab on his bald head, which the doctor had to remove because of his chronic picking, leaving a hole big enough to fit a dollar coin. Every year on the 30th of April, Queen's Day — *koninginnedag* — in the Netherlands, he placed a round orange sticker over it to commemorate her birthday.

His cauliflower nose, which wasn't the result of Mum's passion for pickling, but an overindulgence in whisky (from his mid-sixties) between five and seven, every day of the week.

Our embarrassment when he fell off his office chair, gripping his heart. 'Call an ambulance. Call an ambulance ...' When the medics arrived and lifted him back, they told Mum he wasn't having a heart attack — he was drunk. 'Oh, oh,' she said, not knowing what else to say.

Small things.

My father loved lilies. He repotted and nurtured them year after year, never forgetting the flowers' message — renewal is just around the corner, and the end of one thing heralds another. He loved roses, despite the thorns that became embedded in his skin, blotchy from blood thinners. Sometimes they'd get infected, sending him to hospital for antibiotics.

He also loved tulips, a reminder of the 'home country'. They bloomed the day he died — the day Mum and I Skyped early, before he was due to wake. We discussed how he hated washing and how it had become difficult for her to shower him. 'Just run the shower,' I candidly remarked, 'because he doesn't like wasting hot water!' She took my advice, but he never woke that morning.

King of vegetables. Fat cabbage hearts, *wit goud* asparagus, blow-your-mind green beans, potato mountains, vegetable September, stomp that stink bug. Healthy heart (ironic, because it failed). He lived for all that too.

I was thirteen when my father converted a small green outhouse into a schoolroom so I could fulfil my dreams of becoming a teacher. He cut counters from plastic buckets, bought a blackboard with chalk and attached a church bell outside. Most days after school, I rang it, calling my younger siblings into my classroom so I could teach them — including giving them a good whack over the knuckles with my yardstick, as our teachers had done to us.

My horse, Rusty. How poor my parents were back then, but Dad somehow scraped together £25 so I could live out yet another dream. Then Sundays off we'd go fishing, thermos full, stealing kūmara, borrowing driftwood, lighting a fire, the sweet potato burning our mouths. Seagull shit on our heads.

Small things.

The small things of love I remember.

Back to tulips. The large tubs were black. 'Half dirt, half compost.' Notepad in hand and bags of newly purchased bulbs at his feet, Dad ordered me to fill them. Helping him pot them meant that when his bloomed in a smorgasbord of colours, perfect in their own diversity, I bloomed with them, watching as they exemplified life, surviving the rainy days and opening to the sun. Each one was alike, tall and budded, before it broke into its true self.

'The more you compliment them, the more beautiful they'll become,' he often reminded me.

I would again be touched by life. Touched by him through small things.

Dad sat beside me in the pew of the Catholic church. I can still smell the incense as the priest swung his censer over Kevin's coffin in absolution, declaring him forgiven of all things and asking God to accept him. 'A diamond in the rough,' my father had whispered of my husband.

A few years later, when I explained my brother-in-law's body had been left uncovered for 24 hours in the stinking heat in a Malaysian jungle, Dad's words were simple. 'Be grateful you were born in a gentle country.'

And when Joe broke his neck — when his helicopter crashed into the side of a mountain, the blade decapitating his passenger, our best friend — my father hugged me. 'You will get over this.'

Five small sure words.

When finally I received Joe's clothing from the hospital, full of blood-dried messages and minus one scuffed grey shoe, Dad said, 'You will find it.'

Four small searching words. But always words.

Cigar smoke up my nose, yet now, on each anniversary of his death, we light one of my father's Coronas, pour a whisky and clink, clink. When I close my eyes, I can bypass the polished wood of his box, the shiny appurtenances, the tiny sore on the corner of his mouth, the unshaved look caused by pale, shrunken skin, and see flowers — a red rose, yellow rose, delphinium, orchid. Lily. Tulip! Of course. All coded in pockets of meaning in his vast garden where butterflies hiccuped, flute-throated tūī sang and where mint, and Mum's baked apple, wafted through the air. Any sadness only intensifying happiness. I barely recall the big things in his life. Maybe official grandfather of the New Zealand kiwifruit industry. Pioneer. Farmer. They leave only fleeting memories, fleeting moments of joy, as if they've lost their lustre. They even seem superficial. It's the little gems and their contrasts I'm thankful for.

And it's the small things I now embrace in my own life as it drifts into its final semester. It will be my turn next, then my children's … their children's …

When I flitter in the garden, potting lilies with my newly purchased tulips — in a black tub, half dirt, half compost — I see angels and butterflies, fat bees; I hear the rippling of fine leaves in the trees; I taste drops of sweetness from overhanging Kūwhai. The hedge clipped, weeds pulled, for an hour, for a year — following footsteps.

Not that there isn't any ugliness and pain in the world — I've experienced some. It's that I have learnt what is important in life: what allows me to overcome these things, and what gives me joy. At night, I look back on my happiest memories: words of wisdom, potential diamonds, a gentle country, three sons, the wind combing a gull's feathers, the gurgle of a frothing pool, a magpie's dawn song ...

My story is simple — a sparrow's tweet. It's about bypassing the litter on the roads and seeing the bright colours of life. Of what's most important: of living, love, memory, beauty.

Of small things.

I must live too, get on with what is left of my life. And maybe, just maybe, when my path stops ... at its dead end ... my children, and their children, will plant bright tulips, all shades imaginable, in a black tub, half dirt, half compost.

Ever has it been that
**love knows**
not its own depth
until the hour
of separation.

**KAHLIL GIBRAN**

# FORGIVE ME, I LOVE YOU

## Gail Scarlett

My sister, Dreya, did paperwork. I stared clueless at the crossword. We waited for sounds from our parents' bedroom.

Dad, shattered and confused, slept and emitted loud snores from a goldfish-like mouth. We'd moved your matrimonial bed close to the wardrobes so the hospital bed could fit into the room. Its large, utilitarian 21st century clinical ugliness contrasted with the 1950s coziness you'd come to despise. The side-rails were up to stop you climbing or falling from your narcosis-induced dreams.

Suddenly you were upright and trying to fling one spindly leg over the bed-rail. We rushed in. 'Toilet, I need the toilet,' you whispered frantically. Your usual path was blocked because the bed was crammed against the sliding door leading to the verandah. Gently, we grabbed you and soothingly suggested the potty-chair next to the bed. 'I'm not using that thing,' you snapped and headed for the tiny ensuite. Lit only by the night light, we held you between us as Dad snored on. Fitting three grown women into that tiny space would've had us shrieking with laughter at any other time.

As Dreya held you, I gently pulled down the horrid, sodden pull-up incontinence pants. Immediately, you tried to pull them back up over your skeletal legs, once such 'lovely pins'.

'No, Mum, no,' I cried. 'Let me help you. We need to get them off!' It wasn't till later we learnt of the urinary tract infection that was adding to your pain.

Somehow we got you re-dressed, the bed re-made and you 'settled': the euphemism for adequate pain management. Though I'd worked in hospitals, I eagerly surrendered the job of jabbing you with needles to my ever-practical younger 'Lil Sis'. The tag-team of Dreya and me guarded you overnight as increasing agitation overtook your ravaged body. Exhausted,

Dreya took her turn to rest.

The bitter cold of the Brisbane July night in the un-insulated, half-century old, high-set, fibro-lined family home seeped into my bones. Sat in an armchair in the doorway of your bedroom, I'd wrapped myself in an eiderdown from a single bed in the 'boys' room' to await the dawn vigil.

Suddenly, my skin was heating up. Weirdly my body was hot but the air was freezing. Realization came. The dust-mite allergy of my childhood had been triggered by the dusty quilt. Glancing at your stillness, I threw it off and ran to the bathroom. I stripped off and dragged a wet washer over the red puffy skin. Of course, housekeeping had dived down the agenda in the past four months. I stood, incredulous as I burned but shivered and thankfully found the antihistamine tucked into my wallet. It would have to be Dreya's shift now.

The long wait was over. The palliative care nurse arrived at 9 a.m. as I pulled myself from an antihistamine-induced slumber. She was slight but strong and read the detailed notes we'd made of your care. She had a term for the restless movements of your limbs — nicer than 'death throes'. She looked at us with eyes filled with compassion. 'I think it's time,' she said.

We stared, frightened and uncomprehending. 'I think it's time she went into hospital.' My husband is a surgeon. His work has dominated our lives, my hotchpotch career and our family life. Though often absent, I needed him now to help with this decision to surrender Mum's care. I rang. He answered and said he would come in an hour. The fates had aligned for once so that he could help me ... instead of the rest of the world.

Once a decision is made, activity begins. 'How?' I wondered 'How are they going to get my darling mum down those 20 concrete steps?'

Ambos are a practiced, cheerful breed of doers. The hills and houses of Western Brisbane were a challenge happily met by a contraption that held the patient safely as it 'walked' down the stairs. Strange to say, Mum enjoyed it.

She rallied to the sight of the youthful male and female ambulance officers. Banter and flirting ensued. My sister was going in the ambulance with Mum and Dad. I was to pack the bags, hang out the washed quilt and follow on to the hospital. As the ambos transferred Mum from the stair walker contraption to a stretcher I noticed my husband went to her, bent down, spoke and kissed her gently. In a light-bulb moment, I too realized I should say goodbye until I saw her again — *au revoir*, if you like. During all the busyness of the morning I'd not thought of that. I just wanted her to be safe, to be well and to be okay. Before they lifted my beautiful mother into the ambulance I too went to her and bent my head close. 'Now darling you'll be okay. Dad and Dreya will be with you in the ambulance. I will be there soon. I love you Mum.'

'I love you too,' she whispered back. They were her last words to me. And I felt a profound sense of forgiveness and immense gratefulness.

After they'd all gone I went up the stairs to the home of my childhood. Mum's straw hat lay perched on the table in the sunroom. I burst into tears as I realized she would never wear it again, never come home again. Then I turned my attention to the waiting chores.

Sadly enough,
the **most**
**painful**
goodbyes are
the ones that are
left unsaid and
never explained.

**JONATHAN HARNISCH**

# MARY AMUNDSEN

## Roy Innes

Nineteen-forty-nine. Newfoundland joins Canada. 'God-forsaken chunk of rock, good for nothing,' my father said. He should know nothing all right. Blew his veteran's grant on an equally worthless 160 acres in southern Saskatchewan hospitable only to buffalo grass.

Three crop failures later, he went from land owner to itinerant farm worker. The moves were frequent and each one meant a different school and the dreaded gauntlet for the new kid. Sometimes I was lucky and got beaten in the first fight, settling the whole thing. Other times it took two or three.

And so it was a great relief to me when Father eventually got a city job and we moved to Regina where I expected things to be more civilized, especially day one at school. But at first recess: yet another gauntlet, the only difference being the aura of anger that surrounded it. Understandable, I guess, because the school was filled with immigrants' kids, pissed off at people looking down at them. A lot of Indian kids went there too, and they had it the worst. Dumping on them kept the bottom of the ladder just a tiny bit further away.

Fortunately, it was a one-fight school, a fight that ended after only one punch — my nose — dead centre by the kid elected to do the job, a kid named Danny. He did the strut thing, of course, but when everyone dispersed, he came over to me, and to my amazement, offered me his hanky. All kids had hankies in those days, mine dripping with blood.

'What grade are you in?' he said.

'Six,' I answered, my voice distorted. Nose still bleeding.

'My sister's Grade 6, too. Mary Amundsen. She's in Miss Thompson's class.'

'So am I,' I said.

'You're lucky,' he said. 'Mary says she's the best.'

The bell rang.

Miss Thompson made each of us stand up and say our names. Mary was one of the first and she was the most beautiful girl I had ever seen. Her hair was shiny black and braided into a kind of wreath that framed her face, full lips drawn into a shy smile that melted my heart.

I decided then and there that Danny Amundsen was going to be my very best friend. I invited him to come over to our place after school.

He came only once and didn't stay long. I got the impression he felt uncomfortable. I had no idea why. Our shanty was no better than anyone else's in the neighbourhood.

'Sure good to get a friend so soon,' I said after he left.

'He's a half-breed,' Mom said — like a put-down.

That made me mad. I liked Danny and I was in love with his sister. Mom shouldn't have said that.

A visit to Danny's was totally different, and I went over to his place a lot. I was disappointed that Mary stayed mostly in her room, but when she did come out, it made me feel good all over. She'd give me a smile that went right down to my toes and said 'Hi' in a voice so soft I could touch it.

We had record cold that first winter in Regina. You could hardly tell who was who on the way to school — toques pulled down, scarves up. But Mary never covered her face. She glowed in the cold weather.

My love for her went unrequited. No wonder. I was short, freckled and had to wear wire-rimmed glasses; a toad compared to her. But I liked to think we were friends. Not boyfriend–girlfriend friends, just friends.

Grade 6 was the only year Mary and I were in the same classroom. I still walked to school with her and Danny, but I missed not being able to sneak peeks at her sitting at her desk. No chance at recess either. Girls and boys stayed in opposite ends of the schoolyard, but I could see her sitting by herself, reading usually. I wanted to go over and talk to her in the worst way, but I knew I wouldn't be able to take the teasing.

Summer holidays were fun with Danny. His cousins came down every year from the reserve for Exhibition. They got in free because Indians were automatically classified as exhibitors and since I was even darker than Danny with my summer tan, we followed them unchallenged through the 'Indians only' gate.

Mary never went, which didn't surprise me. We were all too wild for her. But I wished she had. There were girls doing roping and riding and she would have won the Indian Princess Beauty contest hands down. But I guess, being a half-breed she wouldn't have qualified.

Three years went by. I didn't get any more handsome, but she got even more beautiful. We started high school in Grade 9 back then. Danny was a year behind, so just Mary and I moved up. Lot of the Indian kids didn't go at all.

I took this as a great opportunity and offered my services as an escort. Her mother thought it a good idea, but Mary said no. Danny told me later it was for my own good. He'd heard that high-schoolers were really cruel to anyone with Indian blood in them. Best I stick with my own kind. Coward that I was, I did.

I got my nerve up only once after that … at the frosh dance in the school gym. All Grade 9s were required to attend and we did, even Mary. When I saw her, it took away my breath. She had on the most gorgeous dress — red velvet — and her shoes were shiny jet black like her hair. I looked down at my second-hand sports coat where my mom had mended a frayed corner. It stood out like an ugly wart.

I huddled with the rest of the Grade 9 boys, joking and pushing one another, trying not to look over at the girls who were gabbing away pretending not to notice us either. But Mary stood by herself, looking nowhere it seemed, smiling.

'All right, now. First dance. Everyone choose a partner.' Mr Main, the vice-principal.

Every Grade 9 kid's heart hit the floor. None moved. Mr Main, obviously experienced in these situations, had predicted the problem. He ordered all senior students to go grab a frosh and dance. I eased into the background and found sanctuary behind a piece of gym apparatus, but I could still see the dance floor. Everyone was up … except Mary. No one had chosen her.

I beetled around the perimeter until I was by her side.

'Wanna dance?' I said, hoping my voice wouldn't crack.

She smiled, but her eyes looked so sad.

'Okay,' she said.

I should have taken her hand, but my brain jammed up. I just stood there like a post. My one dancing lesson from my older brother didn't include how to start the whole thing. She did it for me. In one smooth movement we were together, and I was dancing with Mary Amundsen.

I was oblivious to everything around me; aware only of the feeling of my hand in hers, the closeness of our bodies and her hair glistening in the lights. We didn't speak. Me, because I was in seventh heaven, and she, probably concentrating on dodging my blundering feet.

Nothing I've ever done since ended so soon.

The music stopped and I became a post again. We stood for a moment, looking at one another. Finally, she said, 'Thanks for the dance.'

I wanted to take her hand. Stay with her. Tell her how beautiful she was … but I didn't.

The frosh boys were stampeding to the sidelines and some dumb instinct sent me right after them. When I'd reached the safety zone, I turned around. Mary had returned to her spot off to the side and stood, as she had before, staring blankly into space. I never saw her again.

I don't remember when I heard, or even who told me, that Mary had killed herself that fall.

There was nothing in my head that understood suicide. I couldn't face Danny. I never went over to his house again. We moved shortly after her death, a big one this time — all the way to the west coast. I was fifteen and blessed with the ability to forget. Hormones surged and girls took on a whole new connotation.

Mary rarely came to my mind. I don't know why; my feelings for her had been so deep. But sometimes, out of the blue, the word Indian comes up, and I think back. I see Mary's face and hear her soft voice. If I don't turn my thoughts away quickly, my eyes get tight and there is an ache deep in my chest.

You can love
someone so much …
But you can never love
people as much as you
can **miss them.**

**JOHN GREEN**

# PIECES OF ME THAT ARE LOST

## Marian Penman

Emigrating is an emotional roller-coaster; the grief of leaving family far away, lifted momentarily by the excitement of discovering a new place, then thrown back down suddenly by a song or an aroma reminiscent of a different life.

In 1982 I moved from England to South Africa, following the dreams of my first husband, leaving behind parents and brothers. I cried every day for two years.

In 2005 I emigrated to Australia, following the dreams of my second husband, leaving behind my adult children and grandchildren. I felt like shredded paper that was scrunched loosely together into a ball, bouncing then falling apart, shreds hanging off until the ball was scrunched back tightly.

Although the family planned to follow us eventually, that was all part of a vague future. Everything seemed so wrong. We accept that children grow up and move away, but parents do not move away from their children.

I had been in Australia a few months, just long enough for the novelty to have worn thin and reality to be dealing me daily blows. Into that state of guilt and grieving came my brother Adrian's phone call to say my father had died. I couldn't take it in.

He was supposed to live forever, so he could always be there with his concern, his strong principles and his sound advice. So many things I didn't tell him. So many times I let him down and disappointed him, yet he never showed it, nor did I ever feel his love had diminished. I never realized he was my role model, so I never told him.

When someone we love dies, we lose that part of ourselves that belonged only to them. We should have been celebrating my father's 90th birthday in September. Instead I had to make the trip alone, into the chill of British January.

No matter where in the world I live, there is a part of me that still belongs in England. A part of me that longs for narrow lanes and old churches, for robins balancing on holly branches, for the crunching sound and woody smell as I walk on golden beech leaves. I wonder if I left part of my heart here, waiting to be reclaimed whenever I returned. As we drove south from Heathrow Airport I felt tendrils of emotions seeking out the roots that lay buried, barely under the surface. In spite of my sadness, I felt a connection with the land, an acceptance of the changes and an uplifting joy at the things that remained as I remembered them.

Rumer Godden, in *A Time to Dance, No Time to Weep*, confessed, 'I am still homesick for the feel of our verandah stone floors hot from the sun, and the warm Indian dust between our toes.' I share her nostalgia for a time that no longer exists.

I did not want to be one of those migrants who spent their time tapping on the window of their past, knowing that window was firmly closed, yet longing for glimpses; for opportunities to be reunited with the person they once were, in a different time, in a different place. Yet life has a habit of nudging me with out-of-context, rose-tinted memories of how happy I was at that time, in that place, be it England, South Africa or Australia. Perhaps I left pieces of myself in all those places, because of course, there were happy times in each of them. My times of homesickness were private moments.

Back in Dorset, my lost years slipped away as I felt myself enveloped in the comfort of the familiar. In spite of the cloud of sorrow hanging over us, my brothers and I laughed over old photos and relived memories, seen anew through each other's eyes.

The day of the funeral I was reminded of how we had made the same journey to the crematorium almost exactly six years earlier after my mother passed away. We travelled in convoy, and when our limo drew up behind the hearse, the funeral director, who had been a personal friend of my father, walked in front of the procession, wearing his top hat and tails, tapping his stick as if in some Dickensian melodrama.

During the cremation, so deeply symbolic of a passing through to another life, I could not help but be smacked in the face by the finality that there would be no more hugs, and no more blue aerogrammes written skillfully in Dad's squiggly handwriting.

But back at my brother's house, the atmosphere improved as the whole family sustained themselves on soups and cold platters while doing their best to deplete Adrian's wine cellar. Thus fortified, we were able to face the thanksgiving service in the afternoon. In contrast to the morning, I found it uplifting as I viewed the church packed with people paying their respects, thankful for their own relationships with my father. I sat between my two brothers with a pile of tissues in front of us. There was a moment when we all reached for the last tissue simultaneously and ended up trying to suppress slightly hysterical giggles. There is a thin line between laughter and tears.

We had no idea where Dad would have liked his ashes scattered, but eventually my brothers and I decided to take him for one last trip to the top of Golden Cap. Golden Cap is a cliff, a mile or so from Adrian's house, so named because of the shape of the hill and the colour of the cliff face in the rising sunlight. The cliff is surrounded by farm land except on the southwest side, which looks out on to the sea.

When we were children, a good Sunday afternoon walk would be a hike up Golden Cap. These days there is a well-trodden footpath, but when we were young there was only a narrow footpath beaten through the bracken. Later Dad threw the challenge to his grandchildren and still managed to race them to the top. Everyone who did the climb received a homemade certificate, long before the days of Microsoft Word templates.

So on an icy January morning, my brothers and I made the trek up the hill, lifted up with memories and weighed down with coffee, brandy and an urn of ashes. It was the end of an era. The loss of a dear parent, advisor, mentor and carrier of all our history. Who would now be able to tell us the names of the people in those old sepia photographs? And who would be able to tell my grandchildren real life-stories of World War II?

I grieved for my children, far away in Africa, saddened that I couldn't be with them to help them cope with their own sorrow. But my plane took me back to Australia, to carry on with my new life there. And we all took another step up the ladder of maturity.

# Hope is like a bird that senses the dawn and carefully starts to sing while it is still dark.

UNKNOWN

# BILLY

## Angela Pritchard

Billy was fifteen years old and working in London in the 1960s. A sprawling, grimy city full of life, full of people, all with their hopes and dreams. Billy was there with his own simple expectations, and I wasn't far away.

Billy served petrol at a city garage. He was proud of his first job, and he did it well. He had come from Ireland with his mother, and was helping by earning money for the two of them.

However, on this day Billy's pride was short lived. On this day petrol spilled over his clothing, there was a stray match, and he was alight. In terror and panic, he did the only thing he could think of. He stumbled from the garage driveway, across the road and fell through the glass door of a café to reach his workmates. They were talking and laughing, but stopped abruptly as they stared in horror.

Billy was on fire. Billy was lacerated. Billy was beginning his death.

An ambulance siren sliced through the London streets.

I was a second-year nurse in the big old hospital to which he was taken. It was full of activity. Nights were as busy as days. Incredible things happened, and sick people got better. I was happy to be a part of it, and I loved the place intensely. I had been with patients when they died, and had witnessed my first birth in the middle of a winter night. After that, I climbed up onto the flat hospital roof in the early morning to reflect on the wonder of a new life. A first breath. A perfect infant. To go up onto the hospital roof was not allowed, but I bent the rules and watched the pallid sun rise over London.

A hospital must seem like a frightening maze of corridors and passageways to patients and visitors. It is a place full of busy people, but when you work in one it becomes familiar. On Billy's terrible morning, staff knew where they were expected to be, including me. I was to go to the sideward of the burns unit where I was to 'special' a fifteen year old admitted from casualty.

I found Billy barely awake.

'Oh Billy, what have you done? I'm here though, kid, I'll take care of you.' Good grief, I was barely nineteen years old myself.

A pale woman in a thin woollen coat seated beside the bed gave me a weak smile. Billy's mother. She twisted an emerald green scarf in her hands and her eyes begged for good news. I had none to offer. She scraped her chair out of my way as I approached the bed to make my efficient nursing assessment.

My care of Billy, along with other ward staff, continued for the next few days. At night, from my own small bedroom in the nurses' home, I could make out the window of the room where he lay. While the shaded light glowed, I knew that he lived on, and I returned each morning looking fresh and capable in my uniform.

Most of Billy's skin was scorched black. The house surgeon carefully slit each side of his charred fingers with a scalpel to release fluid and to give some comfort. Tears ran down all our faces as we shared the pain. We moved Billy as little as possible because he wasn't going to lie there long enough to get pressure areas. We wanted him to be comfortable. Regularly I gave the ordered doses of morphine and finally Billy lapsed into a coma.

His mother's vigil continued too. This gentle unassuming woman sat day and night beside the bed while this care went on. She was quiet and never questioned any aspect of what we did for Billy. Sometimes she laid her face on the counterpane and slept. At other times, she left the room for a short while, always being careful to place her scarf where her son would see it if he opened his eyes. She prayed constantly. I became used to the gentle murmurs she made to her god, and as I recalled my physiology lectures, I knew it was a waste of time.

It took Billy four days and four nights to die. His kidneys finally failed and his organs shut down, which was, for medical staff, the expected outcome. The house surgeon and I gently laid out Billy's damaged body.

For his mother it was the end of all hope. Her beautiful, proud boy was dead. From my own privileged short life, I could only try to imagine her grief and her despair. Had her god failed her? After all those prayers? I was young, and I was knowledgeable, and yes, I was caring but I prided myself on my lack of need for divine assistance for this. I had learnt facts I could accept. A gentle mother was told things she did not want to believe.

I remember now, how I rationalized the whole concept with my friends, other teenage student nurses. The day that Billy died, I said, 'You know something? I don't think I believe in God any more. For four days I have heard a woman pray to God to save her son, and I knew that it couldn't happen, so, how does this work? Do we know things that God doesn't?'

Oh, dear heaven, the conceit, the absolute smugness of youth. How arrogant to assume that her entreaty was only for his recovery. How did I know that her prayers were not for his soul as it prepared to leave this earth? And, what right had I to offer any judgment anyway?

I was, with competence and with care, doing my best for Billy, but looking back I realize that in truth I never really saw his gentle mother, well … not in the way I would if I was part of that drama now. And I know why that was. I couldn't put myself in her place. I simply hadn't had the years of life. Now I could, of course, but I guess I must accept the way I was at nineteen, as truly as I appreciate the way I am at this moment in time.

The way I am at this moment? Life has come its full circle.

I too became that collective mother, and then grandmother, made vulnerable by love of a child. The memory of Billy and his mother makes me feel very humble. What an appalling heartbreak for any parent to experience. And what an outpouring of love and grief through prayer.

I also realize that my own little 'be safe' prayers for beloved children or grandchildren are, in comparison, little more than a simple talisman.

One flesh. Or if you prefer, one ship. The starboard engine has gone. I, the port engine, must chug along somehow till we make harbour. Or rather, till the journey ends.

C.S. LEWIS

# HIS VOICE

## Joyce C. Assen

Rebecca had to admit that of all of Peter's characteristics and traits, the thing she missed the most was his voice. To be sure, she missed other things too: the smell of Old Spice, his laugh that started in his belly and worked its way up his throat, and his habit of teasing her all the time. But it was the sound of his tenor voice she missed the most.

Peter and Rebecca, or Becca as he called her, were married for over 52 years when he passed away suddenly of pancreatic cancer. Three months from diagnosis to death. Not nearly enough time for Rebecca to learn to cope on her own. It wasn't that she was dependent upon him financially; they had both worked, and each of them had a pension. She took care of the household finances for many years, so that wasn't an issue. It was the small things she couldn't get used to. When they golfed, Peter would track her drives for her as she had difficulty doing that. When they were out for dinner or had guests in, he would choose the wine as his palate was far more discerning than hers.

Since his passing, Rebecca learnt to do these things on her own. She also found out that even though time doesn't heal the heartache, it does make the remembering easier to handle. She could think back to the many happy memories she and Peter shared and it would bring a smile to her lips, rather than a tear to her eye.

The other thing Becca missed was not having someone to talk to, especially late at night when she and Peter would lie in bed and talk about everything: the kids, the state of the world, their hopes and dreams. If the truth be known, she missed having someone to just carry on a conversation with. She recalled waiting at the doctor's office and striking up a conversation with another elderly lady who was sitting beside her. The only other people in the waiting room were in their thirties, two women and one man, all busily texting on their phones; no one looked up or acknowledged her presence. When she was called to the examination room, the young man said to her, 'It's nice to hear a conversation again.' Then she realized that is what she also missed, the back and forth, ebb and flow of a conversation.

About five years after Peter's death, Rebecca found herself in a health struggle of her own when she suffered a stroke that left her paralyzed on one side and unable to speak for the first few weeks. Her son and daughter, along with their families, spent hours at the hospital helping to care for her and she knew she should be grateful. Even after she was moved to a nursing home, and regained her speech, she acknowledged that life was never going to be the same; she would never go home, she would never go out with friends for dinner or enjoy card games or golfing again. She missed her old life.

But most of all she found herself missing Peter more than she had in years. Before she was able to keep herself busy during the daytime. Nighttime was always tricky even if one kept busy attending the symphony or theatre; you always had to come home to an empty house and an empty bed. That was hard. Sleeping sometimes was impossible.

One day in late May, the doctor held a consultation with her son and daughter to let them know Rebecca's health wasn't improving. 'She seems to have lost all interest in living,' he told them. He went on to say that the best thing would be to keep her as comfortable as possible and prepare for what was coming.

Rebecca's daughter, Liz, visited her mother the following Sunday as she always did. She found her mom listless and tired, and Rebecca said to her daughter, 'I just want to hear your dad's voice again. I miss him so much.' Liz had a sudden inspiration.

Years before at Christmas, Liz picked up talking books from the card store. These were books with a small tape recorder inside. The idea was that her parents would both record themselves reciting *T'was the night before Christmas* for their grandchildren. The grandchildren loved it and for years those books were always put out on the coffee table during the Christmas season and every night the grandkids listened to one or both of their grandparents reciting the Christmas classic. Those same grandchildren were now grown with families of their own and the books were stashed away in some storage box.

When Liz went home later that afternoon she headed downstairs and started going through boxes. First, she looked in one with Christmas decorations, then she looked in another with photograph albums and such. She hit the jackpot on her third try, for buried at the bottom of a box with old greeting cards she found *T'was the night before Christmas* books. She opened one tentatively, as after all these years she wasn't sure the recording would still work.

Her mother's voice filled the air, 'T'was the night before Christmas' her mom began hesitantly. Liz was thrilled and tried the second book. This time it was her dad's voice.

On Monday, after work, Liz drove back to the nursing home. It was a beautiful summer day with the afternoon sun beating down and fluffy white clouds overhead. She found her mother in her usual agitated state. She had had another sleepless night and was tired and cranky.

'Look what I found, Mom,' Liz said as she sat down in the chair next to her mother's bed.

Her mother just stared at the glitter covered book, without comprehending what it was. Then Liz opened the book and Peter's voice filled the small room. For the first time in months, Liz saw her mom smile. She sat and talked to her mother at some length and when they brought Rebecca a supper tray, Liz got up to go. Her mother called her back and asked her to leave the book beside her on the bed. Rebecca ate very little that evening but, then again, she hadn't had an appetite for weeks.

After supper Rebecca lay back on the bed and closed her eyes. She felt along the sheets for the book and found it. Then she placed it on her tummy and opened it, still with her eyes shut tight. The whole recitation, from beginning to end, took only about two minutes and then silence filled the room, so Rebecca opened and closed the book several times to activate the recording again and again.

The nursing staff came to check her vitals. If they thought it was odd that this elderly woman was listening to a Christmas recitation in the middle of June, they never said anything. They knew that the terminally ill often found comfort in sensory things, be it a soft teddy bear, a song or even a familiar smell like a freshly baked apple pie. The senses often evoke memories of happier times and bring peace and tranquility to those who are ill.

Around 10 o'clock that evening, just as the sun was beginning to set and Rebecca was listening to the book yet another time, she felt another presence in the room. She opened her eyes and there was Peter standing at the foot of her bed. He just smiled at her, held out his hand and said, 'Come on, Becca, it's time to go.' Without a moment's hesitation, Rebecca got up and reached for Peter's hand. She did so without fear. Why should she be afraid? After all, she and Peter were heading home together. The nurses found her lying on the bed with the Christmas book clutched in her hand. The audio loop had long since stopped but it didn't matter. It had provided Rebecca with peace and comfort at the time when she needed it most.

# Take time to do what makes your soul happy.

UNKNOWN

# A BALL OF WOOL

## Alison Giles

It was polyps in her nose that finally took her. A cancer formed. A kind of mesothelioma, they said. Yet, it's more likely her death was caused by the medicines the doctors kept persuading her to take.

The ironic thing about my mother-in-law's death was that she understood the natural world so intimately. That a woman, so nestled in the flora and fauna of her landscape, could have such an ignoble death from the overconsumption of pills. She was quick to remedy the afflictions of the villagers by boiling up herbs and weeds into tonics and poultices, and wise to the planting of wildflowers so that bees would pollinate her kitchen garden. Why then, in her final years, did she put her faith in those who knew so little about her world?

There she is smiling out at me from a retrospective of photographs decorating the walls of the village house. On their wedding day — Blagitsa and Dragan — child-like, natural. And here, in a crossover polka dot dress, a thick belt cinching in the now plump flesh of a recent maternity, perhaps my husband. Heels, handbag and cat's-eye glasses easily a compeer of the glamorous Jovanka Broz of her day. And another black and white image, the family of four, tanned and smiling on a beach in Croatia. Blagitsa stands proudly with arms around the family —

including her husband; it says a lot about the marriage. She wore the pants. Dragan, an optical engineer, sits under the lamplight methodically mending crosshairs from the Yugoslav army's rifles, and fixing watches.

He's quiet, slow, precise. And Blagitsa, singing in the kitchen, beans bubbling on the stovetop, sleeves rolled up to the elbows wiping her brow with flour-talced fingers and frosting her hair white. She teases him, stirs him up, tries to get a bite and he gets angry and frustrated. But there are also wrinkles of passion in their faces. My husband tells me that, as a boy, he looked through the keyhole of the bathroom door to see them bathing together, splashing and laughing.

When they first built the village house — which we have now inherited — she planted every possible fruit tree. They remain as a testament of her love to provide for her family. Six apple trees stand sentinel on the north side of the house, one wrapped with rusted wire. Luckily, the wire hasn't embedded itself into the bark and I manage to cut it free from the trunk, wondering why anyone would do this. I soon learn.

There was a 1-metre high snowfall, a rare occurrence, and the weight of the snow split the tree in two like a zipper. Blagitsa, hearing the crack, rushes out. 'Dragi! Dragi, the tree! Help me!'

And in the dark night wading through hip-high snow they lovingly wrap the tree in cloth and wire and heave the two split pieces together and it becomes one trunk again. It holds fast until the wound heals and welds together like the cut on a finger.

Six months later when there is a shortage of water in the village (because the villagers have been wasteful) she persists in finding some. Clomping through the forest that borders the property and visited by wild cats, wolves and deer, she locates a small spring with a continuous flow and begins to dig. When she has a pit the size of a bathtub she carts small rocks and pebbles from around the village and beds them down into the soft mud. Now she can do her washing. And on the edge of this self-made cistern she sits in the warm morning sun listening to the birds while washing her underwear.

She was, if anything, resourceful to the bone. Next, I spy on the wall a photo of a plump middle-aged woman with her greying hair swept up into a bun. My husband, when in his early twenties, had photographed her whizzing away on her Bagat sewing machine embroidering a napkin. I find her bridal trunk, which she brought with her to Dragan's village when she came with him from her parent's village. Inside are embroidered tablecloths, napkins, doilies, knitted jumpers in various patterns of cables and lace.

She knitted two lace wedding dresses; one as a gift for her own daughter and the other for her first daughter-in-law, my predecessor. I have the chance to hold one in my hands — my sister-in-law's — and marvel at the complexity of pattern. I could never take on such an onerous task. Also, I discover knitted overalls for small grandsons and beanies and gloves they wore in the snow when skimming under the barren apple trees on the wooden sled she had crafted them.

She spun her own wool. I find two balls of her hand-spun yarn amongst the commercial yarns in her knitting basket. I can't throw them out. I take the commercial yarn and place the small odd-shaped balls in their colour order and, having found a rusted crochet needle in her sewing drawer, proceed to make a small knee rug. But I can't crochet the hand-spun. I still have it, waiting to become something.

It's a rough sheep wool. I hold it in my hands and imagine her nimble fingers flicking her spindle sharply clockwise to spin the yarn. There are minute bits of twig and grass and seeds from the fleece of an animal who gave up its wool about fifteen years ago. Some of her fine, dyed hair has fallen and tangled itself into the spin. But the spinning was neat, and consistent and good. Much better than I could ever do.

Photographs in the lounge room show the once fashionable silhouettes gradually transform into floral shifts that she wears like a uniform, an apron, a functional scarf holding the hair out of the way. Her beauty is gone, the hair is wild and unkempt, the crooked teeth and gold fillings poke through a tired smile. Her plumpness becomes skinny ankles in orthopaedic shoes, a shrunken body, stooped, tired and wanting to rest. A cardigan to warm the bones and square-rimmed glasses — with quarter-inch lenses — now help the lustreless eyes to see.

I do miss her, even though I'd never met her. Like an orphan, always wondering what the mother was like. What stories could there have been?

How would my life have been different if that other person were in it? She never knew of me, either. She left the world knowing that her son was very unhappy. Some say she even died the same, after years of never seeing him due to his first wife's jealousy.

❊

I have since plied her two balls of yarn together with my own spindle. I cup the ball in my open hands, inhaling it as if to smell her scent. I contemplate the connection, over the passage of twelve years, between two women who have never met, yet who are so alike in many ways. The creamy-coloured ball of yarn that I tenderly washed in a small basin of water like a newborn child is an umbilical cord. A thread of life from one woman to another over measures of time. This ball of wool is more tangible than anything else she has left behind.

The sweat of her labour is in this ball, her industriousness, her meditations, her frustrations, the conversations she had over her lap with other women as dexterous fingers flicked away, the gossip she heard from the other villagers, the feigned laughter of a badly told joke, the complaints of the weather, the pangs of a full bladder, the grumbles of an empty stomach as she thought about what to prepare for lunch for Dragan. It's all here, in this one ball of wool.

To me, growing old is great. It's the very best thing — considering the alternative.

**MICHAEL CAINE**

# A LONG AND LUCKY LIFE

## Blaine Marchand

'I can't complain,' my mother whispers into the curve of my ear. I am leaning over her as she had stirred and beckoned me over to her side with a twigged finger. 'I've had a long and lucky life.'

Long indeed. She is at the halfway point between 103 and 104. Up until a few days ago, she was walking about with her assured grace. But she has eaten less and less. Being a tiny woman, one fussy about food and with a streak of vanity about her girl-like figure, she always ate sparingly, though there was always room for a sweet. Sometimes, she seemed to sustain herself on candies alone.

My mother was very lucky. In the 1950s and 1960s, at the height of their popularity, she was a perpetual entrant in every local contest. She won and won and won. Thousands of dollars, trips abroad, 100,000 gold bond stamps, furniture, even a motorcycle. Mind you, labels on cans of soup, of diced fruits and vegetables disappeared into envelopes she sealed with a lick and then addressed. People phoned her to ask for advice on how to win. Some called to complain these contests were fixed. How could one person's name be pulled so frequently? She took it all in her stride.

This was something my mother learnt early in life. As toddlers, she and her brother were placed in an orphanage by her mother who, having separated from her husband, decided maternal life was not for her and fled the city. As chance would have it, my mother was taken in by the in-laws of her mother's younger sister. They were an elderly couple with grown children. Although poor, they doted on my mother much to the chagrin of their youngest daughter, who lived at home and waited on her parents hand and foot. She resented this young intruder who was another mouth to feed on an already stretched budget. My mother quickly learnt to manoeuvre around the disgruntled daughter. From an early age, she pitched in, picking strawberries, raspberries and apples in the backyard garden plot. She was always willing to walk across the canal into the well-heeled neighbourhood of The Glebe to families who would pay cash for fresh produce. She was proud to cross back over the Pretoria Bridge, the sounds of nickels, dimes and quarters jangling in her pocket.

Perhaps my mother was happy to go out on these errands or to walk downtown to pay monthly bills as a form of escape. The couple who raised her insisted she stay close to home, to spend her days in the shade of the front verandah. Although my mother never understood why until later, the couple were fearful that her father, returned from the Great War, would come and take her away from them.

The view from the front porch gave my mother a glimpse into the world outside her own. In the summer, luxury boats of Americans would plough the waters of the canal as they chugged toward the hustle and bustle of the city centre. Winter brought skaters circling in figure eights, twirling through falling snow on the cleared patch of ice. Couples, arms linked, glided rhythmically as if dancing. The screams of delight as fur-clad children slid down a toboggan run, careening past her. All through the year, each evening as the sun lowered, seminarians from the nearby college would march two by two, their robes flapping in the wind as they strode. Occasionally in winter, the couple told my mother to open the front door and shout 'Kettle's on.' The house would come alive with the pouring of dark tea, the slurping of milk, clinking of cups, and endless, endless chatter.

But time tarnishes, people age. The Christmas my mother was thirteen, the husband suddenly died. She watched the horse-drawn hearse take away the body of the man who loved to sing with her, who taught her how to select the right wood for the stove, who showed her how to cheat at euchre. Left a widow and with less money coming in, the wife became as strained and severe as the black clothing she wore that day she gripped my mother's hand and let out a whimper when the hearse turned the corner. A taxi waited for the family. It took The Driveway along the canal towards the train station. My mother always remembered it as an intensely cold day.

Shortly after graduating from high school, my mother popped in to visit a daughter of the couple at her workplace, Red Line Taxi. A regular customer came in. He was a buyer for a prestige department store, Charles Ogilvy. My mother, well versed in talking to adults, struck up a conversation with the man. Charmed, he told her to come to see him the following morning and he would hire her.

Her first week was rigorous training, learning to fold dresses and blouses, nestle tissue paper into boxes, arrange the purchased item within and how to finish with a flourish of ribbon.

The store owner's wife was a difficult woman. Salesgirls feared her arrival when the thud of silver cane against the marble floors demanded immediate attention. My mother would lift a padded chair from one of the displays and bring it to her to sit on, regal as a queen. 'What takes your fancy today?' my mother always inquired with a smile and then devoted her time to fetching and showing the latest merchandise, never forgetting to compliment the woman on the final choices. Over the next years, my mother rose from clerk to buyer of women's casual clothing for the store.

In love, my mother was lucky even when unlucky. She fell madly for a college athlete who was as handsome and sharp as his prowess on the field. But in the end, his mother ruled against my mother, a girl of unknown origins. Unphased, she resolved her life would be as a career woman.

But a few months later, the man's cousin, also an athlete, my father, started calling around. The wife of the couple was not pleased. My mother's good job brought in money for the house. On payday, my mother would hand over an envelope with her pay and the wife would give my mother $2 to see her through until the next payday. But my mother was smitten by this man who loved her so intensely. After a period of courtship, often meeting outside the house, they decided to marry. But the wife of the couple refused her permission. 'After all these years, how could you now turn your back on the kindness we have shown you?'

Uncertain what to do, my mother went to the parish priest to seek advice. He reassured her she had been dutiful, that it was her right, as an adult, to marry.

'Simply tell her you will give her the envelope until the end of June. Your salary in July will be yours for the wedding and a new life with your husband. I will support you when she comes to complain.'

A woman could not work once married. My mother had to give up her career. Mr Ogilvy called my mother to his office. Appreciative of my mother's fussing over his wife, of her willingness to be helpful with customers, he gave her an envelope with a large bonus. 'I can't accept this. Only my pay please,' my mother said, and pushed the envelope across the desk toward him. He turned it back. 'No, accepting it would please me.' He knew my mother well.

❋

Eight kids and 44 years later, my father died of cancer. My mother was 68. For the first time in her life, she was independent. She cut her hair from the style my father always preferred. She travelled to places she dreamt about. She made new friends, played cards once a week and went to the casino. She stayed in her own house until she was almost 101. Although never fully accepting the long-term care residence, she welcomed the staff with a smile when they came into her room.

Her children remained her delight.

My mother places her hand over mine. 'I have something to say. God has given you a talent for telling stories. I want you to promise me you will thank Him every day.' I nod my head, eager to please. She falls into a deep sleep.

The next day when I visit, her breath is more ragged. Suddenly she awakes, calls me over. 'Do you remember what you promised me? Will you keep that promise?'

Two days later, she dies after a fall. She had insisted she walk back to her bed on her own.

You've got
to do your
own growing,
no matter
how tall your
grandfather was.

**IRISH PROVERB**

# THE SEARCH FOR
# GRANDPA JOE

## Bruce Manners

Grandpa Joe was my father's father, but I barely knew him. Now, more than 40 years after his death, it's something I regret. If only ...

We had proximity, but we never became close. We both lived in the same small town (population about 500) and only a block away from each other. A two-minute walk, but I was rarely at his house, nor he at ours.

My home town, Port Wakefield in South Australia, is about an hour's drive from Adelaide, the state's capital. Back then, Port Wakefield was a centre for the surrounding farming community and its port used by local commercial fishermen. It was the centre of my universe for twenty years. Now it tends to be a town on the road to somewhere else. It's a place where travellers pause to fuel their cars and themselves, and then continue their journey.

Sadly, there had been conflict between my mother and my father's family. That meant there was little contact with Grandpa Joe, except for the obligatory Christmas morning visit — or if I was with my father when he called in to see his parents. Was it my mother's fault? It's difficult to say now. After her death we discovered she had battled with bipolar most of her life. We knew about the tablets she took, but she never said what they were for. Back then you didn't ask.

Knowing about her bipolar helped explain to us, her children, her at-times erratic behaviour. She wasn't a bad mother and none of us ever felt physically threatened — but there were times when we tiptoed around her to keep the peace. Life was easier if we did.

Looking back, it was what it was and a part of our life as we children grew up. I have only warm thoughts for my mother and sympathy for her struggle with her mind.

Grandpa Joe was a commercial net fisherman. A third-generation fisherman. His three sons were fishermen, but my father was the only one who made it his life's work. I left school at the age of fifteen to work with my father for five years. My two brothers also worked with him for several years. Fishing was in the family. I saw Grandpa Joe more often then, but I was too busy in my own teenage life to want to spend much time with him. Or to have too much interest in what he was doing. For that I can blame no one else.

To find out more about him I phoned Auntie Joan, my father's only surviving sibling, to ask about her father. Auntie Joan is in her late eighties. Her mind is sharp, she still drives her car and cares for grandchildren.

'What was he like? Look at the boys in the family,' she advised. She was talking about the extended family. 'They're all quietly spoken. They are gentle men. That's what your grandfather was like.'

Gentle men? That was true. I'd met a couple of Grandpa Joe's brothers, several of their sons and more of their grandsons — my cousins. There was/is a gentleness about them. She could only recall one incident when she saw him angry and that was when she was a child. Grandpa Joe had told her and her twin brother not to play with the tools in the shed while he was away fishing for the day. He had spent a lot of time preparing and sharpening tools for a woodworking project.

When he returned to find they had disobeyed and a couple of his chisels were chipped … let's say that he was not so gentle.

She told of the only time she saw him cry. It was on my father's eighteenth birthday in 1940. It was war time and my father had to register for military service and Grandpa Joe knew he would be shipped out to Papua New Guinea. My father, another gentle man, was not willing to kill and served as a non-combatant.

The Grandpa Joe I remember wasn't imposing. He was physically strong, but had a wiry frame. His six-foot sons were taller than him. I treasure a large black and white photo of him in his late sixties where he's sitting down mending a fishing net. I would often see him doing that. It's what net fishermen did. He has on his black-rimmed glasses, but what stands out is the jumper he's wearing. It has a couple of holes at the shoulder. I remember that jumper. He wore it often — and for many years. It was obviously a favourite that he wasn't going to let go. I can only imagine what Grandma Muriel thought about it.

He mended his nets when there were holes and tears, why not a little thread for his jumper? I wondered it, but never asked.

My contact with Grandpa Joe tended to be when my father visited him and I would tag along. My early memories are of playing among wood shavings in his shed while they talked about fishing and fishermen or the things they were working on. I have no memory of ever seeing him in his house. Perhaps Auntie Joan was right when she told me, 'He was always in his shed.'

And the smell of his shed stays with me. Yes, the smell of fish was often there, but it wasn't strong. The smell of worked timber seemed to always be there.

He was always working on some kind of project. He built his own boats — something he also taught his sons to do. I'm also aware of a boat he built for one of the garage owners in town. And the local doctor even commissioned him to build a yacht. Apparently, on inspection, the doctor pointed out some flaws in its construction.

'You've noticed some mistakes in my work,' Grandpa Joe is reported to have said.

'What do you do with your mistakes?'

'We put daisies on them,' he replied.

Whatever the flaws, the doctor used his yacht to sail around the Pacific.

There was nothing flashy about Grandpa Joe. He seemed to enjoy the simple life and what he was doing. He became an old man of the sea. He was still fishing alone in his late seventies. At this stage of his life, I remember him motoring in from fishing one day to tie up at the wharf. I asked, 'How did you go today?'

'Just tobacco money,' he said.

He always used words sparingly. Not much more was said. His comment put a positive spin on a poor catch. It was his way of saying, 'I didn't get much, but I got something.'

He may have been a quiet, gentle man, but he could make his presence felt when he needed to. And 'he could be stubborn at times,' confessed Auntie Joan.

Grandpa Joe called around to our house one day when my father had just begun another boat project. He had laid the keel and was preparing for the next steps. 'You've got that wrong,' he told my father. 'You need to pull it apart and fix it here, here and here.' He pointed out where the problems were.

My dad did what he was told. And it fixed a problem he would have had.

What I didn't know, but discovered from Auntie Joan, was that he was also a civic leader and for three years the chairman of the local council. Under his leadership an embankment was built to protect our town from flooding by the little river running on its outskirts.

That made me proud. This gentle man could make things happen. Mahatma Gandhi once said, 'In a gentle way, you can shake the world.' Grandpa Joe may not have shaken the world, but he did get things done.

In the early 1970s, when I married, we shifted interstate for study and work. A couple of years later our first child, our son, was born. We travelled back to Port Wakefield so our family could meet him. Grandpa Joe was in the district hospital, so we went to visit. We took some photographs of the family. In one there are four of us — four generations: my father; me; and Grandpa Joe holding his great-grandson in his arms.

Grandpa Joe died a few months later.

I barely knew Grandpa Joe. Now I wish things had been different. If only I'd taken the time to get to know him. That remains a regret. His tombstone records the details: born 10 July 1891; died 20 December 1974. But Grandpa Joe lives on — not in some kind of mystical or spiritual way, but in a flesh-and-blood family way because the apples haven't fallen far from the tree. Or, to use another term, like father; like son ... like son; like son.

That's how Grandpa Joe lives on.

It matters not who you love, where you love, why you love, when you love or how you love. It matters only that **you love.**

JOHN LENNON

# TRUE LOVE STORIES

## Cliff Fielding

To a young lady called Doris from the Holy Cross Convent School I apologize if I lacked the eloquence to court you well, but I can look back now through the fog of time and remember you fondly. At the time, as our family moved away, I was devastated that this budding romance was being squelched in its formation. You on the other hand may not even have been aware of it. Although I was incapable of expressing words to you at the time, a search through my archives, or rather some dusty folders of scrappy paper, show that I managed to pen these thoughts.

> *If I ever see you again*
> *I will pray at your feet*
> *I will ask for recognition*
> *O, if only we could meet.*

And then there was the girl from the train. Each day we would meet on the trip to the city, forging some kind of platonic romance. She always seemed more grown up than me, more versed in adult things. Briefly, there was a spark. Briefly, I could say I had a girlfriend, but then one after-school kiss and fumble behind the tennis courts later, she lost interest. Did I go too far? Not far enough?

My friend Glenn made the acquaintance of two young ladies. They laughed and bantered and exchanged phone numbers.

It was really such a simple plan. Glenn would pursue Katherine, and I, Julia. Double dates, fun nights out together, best friends dating best friends. Perfect. I called Julia, introduced myself, flirted, had playful banter and the game was on. Except that she toyed with me, seemingly disinterested. Glenn, meanwhile, was having lunch with Katherine's parents, all going exceedingly well. Now, if this were fiction we would be prepared for something to go wrong about now. Interestingly, this being real life, something did go wrong. Glenn changed his mind. He lost interest and asked if I could help out by informing her. What else could a friend do? I gave her the news, then asked her out.

Whirlwind romance. Talked and talked, a perfect match. Glenn was unimpressed.

Nevertheless, even in the face of my best friend's scorn I knew that this was a love like no other, this was real. A love that lasts.

I suppose ten months is quite a feat for a sixteen-year-old romance to last. When it happened I was totally unprepared. Who is ever prepared for the love of their life walking up to them and saying, 'This guy at work has asked me out, and I said yes'?

And I watched her walk away into some kind of phony sunset of older men and cars, and grown-up things.

Being me meant that I carried this rejection for years. I wrote about it, I thought about it, I used it as a filter to observe every subsequent relationship. It had a profound effect upon how I viewed the male–female dynamic and often I would sabotage a relationship because this lurking failure from my teens kept whispering to me 'It won't last, she'll leave'. In the months following, I swore off relationships, said I would never love again and generally performed melodramatic histrionics around the idea of romance.

Years later, she added me on Facebook and apologized. The truth was finally out there. Because she was a few months older, and a whole school year ahead of me, she was constantly hassled by her friends. In the end, she just gave in to it. What could I do but forgive her?

Back then I decided that no way would I let a girl capture my heart again. No way I would fall foul of any young woman's charms. Then one day, wandering the suburban streets there she was, standing on a small patch of grass overlooking the fast-moving automotive glory that is the main road north to Auckland. Blonde hair, slightly tussled by a typically Wellington wind, pale complexion with just the slightest hint of adolescence. Her eyes lit up as she contrasted the small patch of grass we were on with the concrete ugliness of the motorway.

Mary was unlike anyone I had met before. We became entwined in each other's lives. I wrote her love poems, she introduced me to English folk music. She had a gentleness that I've seldom seen again. I pursued her relentlessly; she introduced me to her new boyfriend.

Krissie, I met at Wellington Railway Station and pursued her for around a year, never making much headway until one night, not long after having left my parents' suburban security for a broken-down inner city share house, I conspired to be alone with her. I put a Donovan record on the stereo, slid my arm around her and commenced my not-so-subtle seduction. Although we ended up in my bedroom, my memory is that she seemed particularly bored by the experience. And Glenn was angry because I had not put his record away.

We were a turbulent couple. Me forever declaring my love, and she forever walking out on me. She wrote rambling, blood stained letters, practising self-harm before we even had a name for it.

I remember a party in our share house that had me running through an emotional gauntlet. All evening Krissie had been throwing herself at John, the self-appointed guardian of our household, and so when Mary turned up my spirits lifted until a short time later I saw her slipping away with John to his room.

At the same time, Krissie was making her way down the hall with my best friend. Looking back on it, the entire thing plays like a scene from a Woody Allen film, but at the time I was heading to the kitchen to obtain a frying pan with which to beat my friend senseless.

Later, lying in the dark on either side of our shared bedroom, explanations and actions were examined and absolution given. After all, friendship runs deeper than youthful obsessions and he had only been trying to escape the ignominy of being a seventeen-year-old virgin. That night the template for our relationship was forged. A relationship of grace and forgiveness impervious to human behaviour or differing ideologies.

But the soap opera was not yet over. Forever scheming to get Krissie to myself I arranged a train trip to Auckland for a Joe Cocker concert. We would spend one night with a friend of hers and the next night in a sleeping compartment on the train journey home. No expense was spared for our special weekend away.

As with all Krissie-related events, nothing ran according to plan. Night one, she chose to sleep with her friend, making the following day tense and uncomfortable. Then as we were heading to the train she decided to hitchhike home alone.

The next morning I rolled into Wellington station, the solitary occupant of my sleeping compartment, miserable and defeated. But there was to be one final turn of the knife. She was apologetic, all cuddles and kisses and we spent a pleasant evening together. As we lay there afterwards I thought that maybe at last this was going to work out. At that moment she jumped up and walked down the hallway into John's bedroom.

Alone, her smell lingering in the room, I cried. Love obviously was not for me.

❀

Christmas Eve 1973, late night shopping, wandering, lonely, tortured by this thing I thought was lost love but is more likely to have been a combination of youthful striving and relational dysfunction. A young woman listening to a Salvation Army band playing Christmas carols became my focus. In the real world this sort of thing doesn't usually happen, but on this particular night, in this particular place, everything worked.

Somehow we found ourselves at midnight mass. Crazy, packed, people everywhere, nowhere to sit, the intensity, the crush of the crowd and this young woman Vicki and I suffocating with boredom. First kiss, giggles and tightly held hands as we ran from the place laughing and shouting into the midnight streets. Beginnings of romances are always exciting, everything new, so much discovery. This time it would be different.

Lying in bed the next morning I looked at her and sincerely explained that I was not looking for love. I was finished with that; all I wanted was to enjoy life. Pompously, I warned her not to fall in love with me. This was the new me, casual, enjoying life, not ensnared in some female flight of fancy.

Of course, I had sabotaged myself. The day came when she lost interest and went on to other adventures. She had taken me at my word and not fallen in love; unfortunately, I had betrayed myself and fallen in love with her.

It would be another twenty years before I realized that my problem was not falling in love with too many women. My problem was that I was in love with falling in love.

At sunset the
**little soul**
that had
come with the
dawning went
away, leaving
**heartbreak**
behind it.

L.M. MONTGOMERY

# THE PRESENCE OF AN ABSENT CHILD

## Evanthe Schurink

Her presence, and the wonder of being blessed carrying life for a second time, came as quite a surprise. In fact, everything about her was a surprise. I will never forget her first movement; it wasn't a shy fluttering like that of her sister, but a strong kick. Once she started kicking she did so non-stop as if announcing: 'Watch out world, here I come!'

I couldn't wait to hold her in my arms seeing what she looked like, but at the same time I also wanted to keep her just where she was, safe inside me.

From her first cry leading to the nursing staff nicknaming her Maria Callas, she managed to head-over-heels turn the world upside down. She looked so fragile, like a porcelain doll, with her black hair curled on top of her head, her pouting mouth and eyes looking directly into my soul. I stared at her in awe. She had no resemblance to any family member. No one could claim that she looked like one of them. She just looked like her perfect self, and I knew that even though our entangled lives ended, she would always be part of me. I looked at her curly toes and wondered where those little feet would walk. Little did I know, as I held her so close to my body that it almost felt as if we were one again.

Through the months she didn't only grow under my heart but as her sister, deep inside it. I thanked the Lord for her and for being a mother and, as if I knew what was coming, I prayed that He would send a very special angel to keep her from harm. She gave her first cry while being born, as if she couldn't wait to announce her presence to the world. From then on, she lived to the full, tumbling from one moment into the next, as if she couldn't wait to take the world by storm. Crawling at six months and climbing over her cot rails at seven months. Then the big surprise when she was nine months old, finding her standing on top of the dining room table with a big smile on her face, looking so proud, while I nearly fainted. Fortunately, with each daring venture her guardian angel protected her.

From the moment she could move on her own two legs she never walked but ran, jumped and danced. No wonder, then, when she started talking one of her first sentences was 'Look Mommy, look!' as she showed me a new trick.

She could be a real little lady, loving to dress in lace and ribbons and dancing on the tips of her toes but was as happy climbing trees. She was my bright starlet twinkling from afar and a loving kitten curling up on my lap. A rivulet babbling its way over cobbled stones. One minute she was a butterfly showing her beautiful colours and the next she was quietly sitting in a corner drawing pictures. However, she could also be as fierce as a tiger protecting the weak. She rushed through our lives like a little hurricane, changing everything, but making everyone love every moment with her in it.

I remember the day when she was about four years old and her sister called me to come and see what she was doing. Shocked to the bone, I saw her trying to balance herself on a washing line she'd somehow spanned between a pile of bricks and the wall about 3 feet off the ground. I took her in my arms and carried her home, praying to God that He must please protect her when undertaking her crazy ventures.

But it was no crazy venture that took her away from us. It was the horror of bone cancer, that despite all our visits to the doctors was only diagnosed after it had already spread throughout her body. Because of her joyous nature, nobody knew how sick she really was or that the seed of destruction was already planted in her and was starting to bloom. She was but ten years old, just becoming aware of herself, not only as a girl with a mind but as a little lady with class parading in front of the mirror.

She was so gracious and strong, but cancer came and changed everything. What hurt most was that she had to face the degrading changes to her blossoming body that the cancer and chemo brought. After the operation removing the main tumour, she was like a broken doll who hardly ever smiled and never again jumped and danced, but just faded away. Still, like a child I never stopped believing that a loving God would not let her die.

As her agony became worse, especially during her last days on Earth, I could no longer bear seeing her like that. I cried throughout the night, holding her aching body fighting to stay alive close to mine, like when she was a baby. I imagined us again as one, but

I could not hold on. I could not save her from harm as a mother should — no one could but God.

In the early hours of the morning of the last day, she melted away into complete peace, sliding through my fingers like water.

Then she was gone, like sand flowing through the hour glass of life, never to return. I lost my precious little girl and I was losing my mind. I was devastated and couldn't believe that my prayers hadn't been answered. How could my heavenly Father, whom I trusted, take her away? The pain of putting her in that white coffin in a black hole was excruciating. The agony of leaving her, my little girl, who was so scared of the dark and of being alone, was sheer anguish. It was springtime, blossoms bloomed all around me, but inside me everything was dark and dead. How could I go on without the part of my body and spirit that I loved so deeply? I knew I had to pull myself together, because as well-meaning friends reminded me, I had three other children to care for and a husband.

I soon realized that the path of grief is the loneliest path anyone can ever walk on this earth. We stopped mentioning her name (and after 34 years seldom do) for fear of hurting each other. My friends, those I still had, kept encouraging me to move on. How could I explain to them that I could never move on, because part of me had died with her? How could I tell anyone how angry I was at God for taking her away? I ended up shutting the curtains of my soul, so no one could see the pain and the agony of my longing to hold her in my arms and the desperation of not being able to do so. I became quite good at wearing a mask, pretending that everything was fine. I became two mothers: one lived, like a moth, in darkness, caught in the shadows of the past. The other, the day mother, was merely existing, going through the motions of caring for my children and husband just to return to my suffering when I was alone at night.

One night, years later, I had a dream of me and her walking along the beach with Jesus. She was on His right side and I was on His left. Although I knew that she was there I couldn't see her, but I heard her laughing her happy laugh. I experienced an intense feeling of peace as I became aware that she was not taken away from me, she was still walking with me but just on the other side of Jesus. When I woke up the next morning I had the intense desire to put my hand to paper and let my caged emotions free. I finally had a way of talking to her, about her, writing her name and pouring out my sadness. As I wrote verse after verse I felt the burden of loss lifting and through the light of peace I transcended my sorrow.

Slowly through the days, months and years that followed, the black moth transformed to grey and red and blue and yellow, becoming a multicoloured butterfly celebrating her life, bringing a message of hope to other grieving mothers. Not that I have no bad days — there are still days when I creep back into the darkness of my longing for her, times when I hear her calling me 'Look Mommy, look!'

I have accepted that I will never be able to move on and be okay without her. Her absent presence will always be with me. I know one day I will move on, but to the other side, where we will meet again. Knowing her, I am sure that she will have a mind-boggling surprise waiting for me.

**Love** alters not with his brief hours and weeks, but bears it out even to the edge of **doom.**

**WILLIAM SHAKESPEARE**

# UNSPOKEN LOVE

## Pamella Laird

It was October 1945.

Forty-two-year-old Laycie's whole body stiffened when two arms suddenly enveloped her from behind. To her joy and relief when she twisted around, she found the arms holding her so ardently were those of her husband.

In an instant, three-and-a-half unspeakable years had gone forever. A disbelieving smile lit her face as she held Richard's haggard face between her trembling hands. For so many years she had longed only that they be together.

At Southampton two hours before, her skeletal legs almost useless, she'd turned to thank the Red Cross nurse who had helped her onto the train. The nurse's snowy veil wafted like the wings of an angel in the chilly breeze. Even then, Laycie's knees fluttered like aspen leaves in a breeze as she settled into the compartment to face the weary journey to Waterloo.

Remembering her school days, Laycie braced herself for the last 65 miles. Today, on the tail end of wartime conditions and erratic timetables, most likely she was facing a trek of well over two hours. Would a nurse be on board to keep an eye on her and Laycie's hundreds of fellow travellers — each with their own nightmare thoughts of the past and fears for the future?

Wrapped in a khaki blanket, in her lap she gripped a small drawstring canvas bag holding a comb, a hairbrush, toilet bag, a tin pannikin, a metal spoon, a shapeless nightgown and the almost new blanket. After the signing of surrender by the Japanese army in Singapore, the Red Cross had distributed basic items to the pitiable prisoners they'd found in such deplorable conditions. Fingers trembling, she pulled at the cords of the bag, groping for the comb to settle her dry, colourless hair. Once chestnut, it was now faded and thin, and months ago had lost any thought of a wave. Previously she had only seen herself in the lid of a tobacco tin discarded by one of the prison guards; even now, a mirror reflected sunken cheeks and yellowed eye whites.

As the train moved into the countryside she noticed hawthorn trees close to the tracks. They dripped with the filmy tears of a damp, drizzly day. But it was all so green! A woman wearing a heavy overcoat and a scarf tied under her chin pushed a deep-bodied, small-wheeled pram along a lane near the railway line. Laycie hadn't seen a coat for as long as her troubled mind could recall. Three-and-a-half years of incarceration on Singapore had left her senses both fragile and hard-edged. First by the grim necessity of staying alive and second by the brutality of despair so cruelly thrust upon her. In the daily challenge of prison awfulness, she'd never dreamed that conditions back in England might also be desperate.

Today she'd wrapped her gaunt shape in the clothing of an unknown Singapore woman who could have been any size or height. Although faded and worn, the two-piece sarong *kebaya* of tropical cotton was clean but miserably inadequate for an English autumn. Laycie pulled the ill-fitting top closer around her chest.

Glancing at the women beside her, she saw only mirror images of herself. All seven clutched similar cotton bags; she smiled to those who caught her eye. Opposite, a young ashen-faced lass half hidden in her army blanket plucked fretfully at a stitched edge. Tormented eyes peered from her blanket cocoon. As she settled back into her seat Laycie's most troubled thought was, 'Will I be strong enough to get from the train to my school-day meeting place on the Waterloo concourse?' She pictured stumbling alone to her 'private island of golden light' near platform twelve. It seemed an impossible challenge.

Beside her, a young woman crooned Brahms' Lullaby to herself. Tears ran unchecked down her cheeks; had she lost a child, perhaps a young baby? The little song went on and on and on. Laycie reached for her hand.

A few weeks earlier, when released from the women's prison by sickened and disbelieving British authorities, Laycie had weighed a little over 5 stone. For two months she'd been hospitalized in Singapore, partly to help her regain her health, but also to wait for a flight or ship's berth to get her back to England. With meticulous medical care she'd gained almost a stone; huge progress from her skeletal arrival at the hospital, but not nearly enough to restore wasted leg muscles so that once more she would be free and independent.

For nearly fifteen months Laycie and husband Richard had been incarcerated in Changi prison, but from the first day, husbands and wives were callously separated. However, worse was to come. In May 1944, women and children were moved 15 miles west to Sime Road prison. For the remaining eighteen months in separate prisons, the women heard nothing of their men. Considering their own conditions, for all they knew many may have died. Even after the surrender in September 1945, neither had any knowledge of the other's wellbeing. Would they ever meet again? Had the other survived the cruelty and starvation that for so long had been their agony to endure? What would happen to them, now they were back in England?

During her years of imprisonment, Laycie had spent the time supporting the women around her, especially those with children, as she had none of her own.

Her eyes ranged over the sweeping fields: here a steeple, there a tower. Through eyes conditioned to the malice of a plant-free, beaten earth compound, the soft colours were balm to her hungry eyes and soul. Was this really her homeland? She'd forgotten the gentleness of the rounded fields now stark in their autumn stubble and the impact of cold in contrast to the island humidity. Had her family been informed of her return? With Britain reeling from five years of deprivation and war destruction, communication was difficult. Therefore, informing relatives in the United Kingdom of their missing family members' arrival would be extremely difficult, if not impossible.

As a teenager Laycie had boarded at school in England. At the end of term her mother's sister would meet and transfer her to and from the boat train. Then, she'd claimed a sunny place by platform twelve where shafts of sun broke through a hole in the hugely curved glass roof of the iconic station. Here she waited in a puddle of golden light for her Aunt Janet to find her. This arrangement solved the worry of meeting up in the hustle and bustle of porters, the hissing of steam engines, plus the general commotion of farewells, greetings and the whereabouts of one's suitcase.

Now totally exhausted, she had given no thought as to who might meet her, what she would do? Maybe the repatriated women would briefly remain in the care of the Red Cross? She smudged away a tear with the back of her hand.

After two hours travelling, she stood at last, in her sunny spot, once more back on her familiar patch of safety. She sighed — was it enough to be home? A rush of cold air swept towards her as a second train pulled into the adjacent platform. Old memories stirred with the soot smell, the rush of steam and the 'barra boys' yelling of their wares to those bustling, unhearing around them.

Laycie's knees folded the moment she'd been grabbed from behind. Then came the overwhelming joy when she'd recognized Richard. Only his instinctive grasp saved her from collapsing. They stood supporting one another; speechless for the long minutes it took for both to realize they'd been on the same train and were at last reunited.

To her horrified eyes his condition seemed worse than her own. In the following years, in raw and anguished moments, Richard would tell of his own wretched months on the Burma Railway.

Through tears of fatigue and relief Richard slung the blankets over one shoulder and grasped her pathetic little bundle along with his. With an arm around her waist, he tenderly supported her towards a nearby flower barrow packed with violets. The 'barra boy' stood beside his rustic cart. The barrow was a deep wooden box stood on two wooden legs, its two wheels reminding Laycie of stylish prams she'd seen when a young girl. Richard chose a posy and handed it to her. She dipped her head into the charming scent of sweetness and love. Richard called, 'How much for the lot — the barrow too?' Laycie giggled. The boy removed his soft cap, saluted and replied 'Sir, ya can 'av the lot for 'arf the usual.' Paper money changed hands and following Richard's instructions, the young barrow owner wheeled the contrivance towards the guard's van on platform eleven.

Step by step alongside the boy and his barrow, the radiantly happy exiles were enveloped in the delicate scent of the tiny flowers.

Nobody can
do for little
children what
grandparents do.
Grandparents
sort of sprinkle
**stardust**
over the lives of
little children.

**ALEX HALEY**

# THE QUILT

## Anne Hofland

I pull back the quilt and slip underneath it for a nap. My tired muscles relax after a morning spent painting the cottage windows. Gradually I come to feel its weight on my body, the way it curves around my hips and shoulders, lays cozily over my feet.

The quilt is a cherished reminder of my grandmother. She made one for each of us, her five grandchildren, presented at Christmas in the year that we turned nine. Mine is a fluttering, airy display of butterflies, shades of yellow and gold on a creamy background, every stitch sewn by hand. The body of each butterfly is a solid shimmer of golden thread, the four wings fashioned from two different yellow floral fabrics. When I lift up the bottom corner, the words 'Anne 1965' are carefully stitched in the same golden thread. It was the pride of my bedroom as a child, emanating colour, light and love.

When I moved away from home, and no longer had a single bed, I packed the quilt away in a box, where it languished for decades, moving with me from place to place. A few years ago, I rescued the box from the basement, and now the quilt graces the single bed in the guest room at the cottage. Each time I pass the doorway and catch sight of it, it makes me smile. Occasionally I like to nap there, just to admire and enjoy it after all these years.

On this day, I sigh contentedly and sink deeper under the weight of its heavy cotton. It is solid and comforting, exuding a sense of substance and durability as well as beauty. It envelopes me once more in the warmth and love of my grandmother. Even though she has been gone for 30 years, I still miss her.

As I drift off to sleep, my mind wanders back in time. I find myself remembering the September evening long ago when I stepped off the bus in Toronto's west end to see my 75-year-old grandmother standing anxiously on the dark street corner, scanning the faces of the disembarking passengers. Something was wrong. I rushed over.

'Grandma, what is it?'

Her face crumpled and she hugged me close.

'There you are!' she cried. 'I've been so worried! You didn't come home and you didn't call. I didn't know what had happened to you!'

I hugged Grandma back, apologizing for my thoughtlessness. I was living with her while I attended my first year of university, and that night I had stayed downtown studying with friends. I took her arm and we walked home together, around the corner to the sturdy little brick house my grandparents had built. I never forgot to call again.

The fact that Grandma still had the capacity to love was a testament to her character. During the five years that I lived with her, she would often invite me to have dinner, so that I could spend more time on my studies instead of cooking. Over those homemade meals, she imparted snippets of her life that I pieced together to form a portrait of her, stitching together the quilt of her life.

Grandma was always reluctant to reveal her true age, but I found out that she was born in 1898. She grew up in Toronto with her parents and three siblings. As a child, she was left-handed, but at that time this trait was considered a sign of the devil, so in school her left hand was tied behind her back to force her to use her right. She told me that as a girl she could run like the wind. I loved to picture my matronly grandmother as a young girl in full flight, hair flying behind her. It was undeniable that she had passed that athleticism on to my father and then to me.

Her adulthood had started with great promise. She and my grandfather had married and built their home together from the ground up. It was a small but handsome house, a source of great pride, and she still had the bills for every nail that had ever been put into it.

I knew that Grandma's life had been beset with tragedy and hardship. My grandparents had lost their first child, a daughter, to diphtheria at the age of seven. My dad was born soon afterwards. Two years later, my grandfather deserted them both, never to return nor to offer a penny in support. Grandma became a single mother in the 1930s, a situation which must have been devastating for her, emotionally, socially and economically.

Grandma took in boarders for years, dividing the small house into three apartments. She and my father lived on the ground floor, where she had a kitchen, a living room, and a dining room converted into a bedroom. They shared the bathroom in the basement with the downstairs boarder.

But there were additional hardships in my grandmother's life that I never knew about until well after she died. I learnt much later that before my grandfather filed for divorce, Grandma transferred title of the house into her parents' names to keep from losing the roof over her head. But then they refused to sign it back to her. She was forced to take legal action against her own parents, and to buy back the house from them. To make ends meet, Grandma worked many different jobs. A talented seamstress, she took in sewing. She worked in a factory, became a practical nurse. But the only job that I knew of, and the best job in the eyes of her young grandchildren, was at Hunt's Bakery.

There would always be treats when we visited, or when she babysat, which was often. My brothers and sisters and I spent weeks with her in the summer at the tiny cottage on Lake Simcoe that she inherited from her parents.

When we were old enough to go to university, four of us took turns living with Grandma while we studied downtown at the University of Toronto. She only ever asked us for enough money to help her pay the bills. Although she had lived a life of enforced frugality, she was always as generous with us as she could afford to be.

Grandma stayed in her beloved home until she was 86, when a series of strokes necessitated the move to a nursing home. I visited her there regularly, and although her mobility deteriorated and eventually she was confined to a wheelchair, she remained alert and talkative, and was always interested in the events of my life. When she was 89, I found out that she had never been to a drive-in movie, so my partner and I were planning to take her to one the following summer, but she passed away in March, and never made it to the drive-in.

Not surprisingly, it was Grandma's heart that finally wore out. She simply slumped over in her chair one day, dying immediately and painlessly. After the travails of her 89 years, her death may have been the only thing that ever came easily to her.

❀

When I awaken from my nap that summer afternoon at the cottage, I lay still for a while, savouring the memories that have been evoked. I realize that when Grandma made my quilt, she would have been just a little older than I am now. I silently thank her, not just for the quilt, but for all of the other gifts she gave me that have never been clearer than in this moment — resilience, determination and, most importantly, the capacity to love. Despite the loss of a child, her husband's desertion, her parents' betrayal, she never became bitter. She still found it in her heart to love us, teaching me that the capacity to love comes from the heart, from one's character, and not from the circumstances that life deals out.

I slip my arm out from under the quilt and trace the stitching with my finger, marvelling at the workmanship that has held up over all these years, and at the number of hours it must have taken to complete. With the perspective of age and time, I can appreciate it far more now than I ever did as a child. I know that Grandma would be delighted and touched that it has found a treasured place in my life again.

I smile, picturing her on her rocking chair in the living room, squares of fabric laid out around her, stitching away while she watched television. It is a reminder not only of Grandma's life, but also of a bygone era in the world, a time when scraps of fabric were carefully saved, when sewing was done by hand, and when love was demonstrated by homemade gifts. I have never in my life, before or since, received a gift from anyone that was such a labour of love.

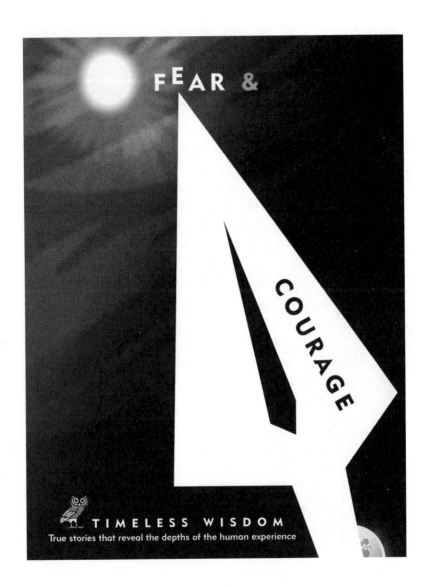

FEAR & COURAGE

ISBN 978-1-925820-06-5

SUCCESS

STRUGGLE &

TIMELESS WISDOM
True stories that reveal the depths of the human experience

STRUGGLE & SUCCESS

ISBN 978-1-925820-08-9